VOICES OF PENTECOST

Voices of Pentecost

Testimonies of Lives Touched by the Holy Spirit

Vinson Synan

VINE
BOOKS

SERVANT PUBLICATIONS
ANN ARBOR, MICHIGAN

Vine Books is an imprint of Servant Publications especially designed to serve evangelical Christians.

Servant Publications—Mission Statement
We are dedicated to publishing books that spread the gospel of Jesus Christ, help Christians to live in accordance with that gospel, promote renewal in the church, and bear witness to Christian unity.

Scripture verses are taken from the King James Version.

Published by Servant Publications
P.O. Box 8617
Ann Arbor, Michigan 48107
www.servantpub.com

Cover design: Evelyn Harris

03 04 05 06 10 9 8 7 6 5 4 3 2 1

Printed in the United States of America
ISBN 1-56955-283-5

Library of Congress Cataloging-in-Publication Data

Synan, Vinson.
  Voices of Pentecost : testimonies of lives touched by the Holy Spirit / Vinson Synan.
      p. cm.
Includes bibliographical references.
  ISBN 1-56955-283-5 (alk. paper)
  1. Pentecostalism. I. Title.
  BR1644.S967 2003
  270'.092'2–dc21

                                                            2003000246

*D*edication

To our wonderful grandchildren

Lauren
Rebecca
Elizabeth
Justin
Lilly
Preston
Priscilla
Chad
Amelia

May your voices be added to
the great cloud of witnesses.

Contents

Introduction / 11

St. Augustine / 15
Thomas Ball Barratt / 17
Frank Bartleman / 20
Dennis Bennett / 22
Reinhard Bonnke / 24
William Branham / 27
Harald Bredesen / 29
J.W. Buckalew / 32
Howard Carter / 35
G.B. Cashwell / 37
Oswald Chambers / 39
Florence Crawford / 41
Gerald Derstine / 44
John Alexander Dowie / 46
David du Plessis / 49
William H. Durham / 52
Charles Finney / 55
Alice Reynolds Flower / 58
St. Francis of Assisi / 60

7

Billy Graham / 62

Elena Guerra / 67

Madame Jeanne Guyon / 70

Kenneth Hagin / 72

Jack Hayford / 74

G.T. Haywood / 77

Nickles J. Holmes / 79

Willis C. Hoover / 82

Edward Irving / 85

Benjamin Hardin Irwin / 88

Stephen Jeffreys / 90

Pope John Paul II / 93

Joseph H. King / 95

Kathryn Kuhlman / 98

Joan McCarthy / 101

Francis MacNutt / 102

Aimee Semple McPherson / 105

Asa Mahan / 108

Patti Gallagher Mansfield / 111

Dwight L. Moody / 113

Jennie Moore / 115

Dan T. Muse / 118

David Wesley Myland / 120

Agnes Ozman / 122

Charles Parham / 125

Jonathan Paul / 128

Pope Paul VI / 130

Lewi Pethrus / 133

Pandita Ramabai / 136

Kevin Ranaghan   / 138
Oral Roberts   / 141
Pat Robertson   / 143
Mark Rutland   / 145
William J. Seymour   / 148
Demos Shakarian   / 151
A.B. Simpson   / 153
Barton Stone   / 156
A.J. Tomlinson   / 159
John Wesley   / 161
Smith Wigglesworth   / 164
J. Rodman Williams   / 167
Maria Woodworth-Etter   / 170

Sources   / 173

*I*ntroduction

This book exists at the suggestion of Bert Ghezzi and my good friends at Servant Publications. The first time I had breakfast with Bert many years ago, he suggested that I write a book on pentecostal-charismatic history. I outlined the chapters for a new book on a napkin that ultimately became *In the Latter Days*.

This small, popularly written history was successful far beyond our dreams. It has been published in more languages than any of my other books. Its influence has truly been worldwide.

For *Voices of Pentecost*, the model was Ghezzi's *Voices of the Saints*, a recent book with 365 daily devotional readings from the great saints of the church, one for each day of the year. My book, he explained, should accomplish something of the same thing with readings from the heart of the pentecostals and charismatics who now make up the second largest family of Christians in the world after the Roman Catholic Church.

In the process of planning a book such as *Voices of Pentecost* I immediately began to think of what would be appropriate to include that would be valuable to scholars and popular readers alike. I settled on the idea of including firsthand testimonies from a variety of people from all segments of the pentecostal and charismatic movements. Since the movement just ended

11

its first century in 2001, I felt that it would be important to include testimonies from some of the "pre-pentecostals" (those persons before 1901) who were clearly in the lineage of the Catholic/Anglican/Methodist/Holiness streams of Christian spirituality. I therefore included testimonies from such persons as St. Francis of Assisi, St. Augustine, John Wesley, Edward Irving, Charles G. Finney, D.L. Moody, and others.

Many of the pentecostal testimonies are from leaders of the twentieth-century pentecostal movement, including such well-known persons as J.H. King, A.J. Tomlinson, Aimee Semple McPherson, and William J. Seymour. Along the way I added some wonderful testimonies from largely unknown persons such as the Church of God Evangelist J.W. Buckalew. The saddest part of the project was that dozens of fantastic testimonies had to be excluded because of space constraints.

Most of the testimonies are concerned with such pentecostal events as baptism in the Holy Spirit, speaking in tongues, divine healing, and the like. The later testimonies of charismatic leaders such as Pat Robertson and Gerald Derstine differ little from those who are now called "classical pentecostals." The testimonies from the Episcopal, Presbyterian, and Catholic charismatic movements indicate some differing nuances and shades of theological understanding. But all in all, there seems to be an amazing unity in the witnesses to the manifestations of the charismatic gifts of the Spirit.

Of course, it is beyond the scope of this book to verify all the claims of divine healing or speaking in known languages. This book concerns what the pentecostals and charismatics experienced and believed as reported in their own words and according to their own understanding. In the end, these people passionately believed in what they saw, heard, and experienced. The reader may choose to believe that these testimonies are genuine, to question them, or to see them as the misguided results of religious zeal.

Whatever one thinks, however, it is true that the belief system and experiential dimensions of the following testimonies have produced the most buoyant and fast-growing Christian movement of the last thousand years. David Barrett, a Christian missions statistician, has estimated that by 2002, all the pentecostals and charismatics of the world taken together, found in all denominations, numbered some 620,000,000 participants worldwide. This book contains samples of the more-or-less typical testimonies of these people. And, although the number of testimonies could be multiplied by the thousands, time and space will permit us to use only the sixty-one chosen for this book. Perhaps a reading of these testimonies will enable inquirers to gain a better understanding of the beliefs, experiences, and lifestyles of these people who are now so widely spread around the world.

As usual, my wife, Carol Lee, has been indispensable at every stage of producing this volume. Her typing, editing, and proof reading have been of the highest quality. Also, I salute Bryan Carraway, my Graduate Assistant at the Regent University School of Divinity. His search and research in the early stages of the book were a great help to me.

Vinson Synan
Regent University
Virginia Beach, Virginia
July, 2002

St. Augustine

"The people shouted God's praises without words, but with such a noise that our ears could scarcely stand it."

St. Augustine (354–430) is considered to be the greatest of the early church fathers. His writings laid the foundation for Christian thought and theology. He spoke passionately about the validity of the faith and labored hard to expose and destroy early heresies that were sneaking into the church. He left behind more than a hundred books, five hundred sermons, and more than a hundred letters as well. Both Catholics and Protestants look to him as a father in the faith.

St. Augustine was born in A.D. 354, in the North African town of Tagaste. As a youth he lived for pleasure and sought answers to life's problems through secular philosophy. One day while meditating in his garden he heard a voice speaking to him saying, "Take up and read." He picked up his Bible and opened it to Romans 13:13-14. What he read pierced his soul, and he there began his journey toward God. He was ordained a priest in 391, and in 396 he was made the bishop of Hippo.

St. Augustine recorded many miracles that occurred while he was bishop of Hippo. We get a glimpse of what it must have been like to be a member of his congregation in fifth-century

Africa in an account of the spontaneous praise that burst forth when one such miracle took place. The following description of St. Augustine in prayer seems reminiscent of early pentecostal prayer and healing meetings that took place in the early part of the twentieth century.

You will see him singing with intense emotion, with the expression of his face adapting itself to the spirit of the psalm and with tears often coursing down his cheeks. He sighs between the words that he sings, and whoever has no special skill in reading men's thoughts will be wholly taken in by the outward appearance and will say: "How deeply this lad is stirred as he listens to this psalm!"

See how he sighs, how deeply he sighs.—And then the man in his turn begins again to sing and puts into the song all the power that is in him. Yes, he sings with the very marrow of his bones, with voice, face and profound sighs all showing how deeply he is stirred.

Although St. Augustine was the first theologian to state a cessation theory in regard to miracles, he soon had to change his mind. One year on Easter Sunday, a notable miracle took place in his church in Hippo. A young man named Paulus was healed of convulsions before the eyes of the congregation. The next day his sister Palladia was also healed. The following description of the moments just after the healings is one of the most vivid scenes in all the literature of the early church fathers.

Then everyone burst into a prayer of thankfulness to God. The entire church rang with the clamor of rejoicing.

Augustine took the young man in his arms and tenderly kissed him. The congregation had a similar response the next day when Paulus' sister was healed in a similar way. Augustine continues his eyewitness description:

Such wonder rose up from men and women together that the exclamations and tears seemed as if they would never come to an end.... [The people] shouted God's praises without words, but with such a noise that our ears could scarcely stand it. What was there in the hearts of all this clamoring crowd but the faith of Christ, for which St. Stephen shed his blood?

Thomas Ball Barratt

"I burst out in a wonderful baritone solo."

Thomas Ball Barratt (1862–1940) was born in Albaston, Cornwall, England. His life, and the lives of millions of others, was forever changed because he once happened to be in the right place at just the right time.

When he was age five Barratt's family immigrated to Norway from his native England. He later felt God's call to ministry and in 1889 was ordained a deacon. Two years later he was ordained as an elder in the Methodist Episcopal Church of Norway.

At age forty Barratt founded the Oslo City Mission. Four years later, in 1906, he made what he thought would be an uneventful trip to the United States to raise money for the Norwegian Methodist Church. He had no idea that this trip would change his life and shape the destiny of an entire continent.

While he was in New York someone asked Barratt whether

he knew that a revival was taking place on Azusa Street in California. He replied that he had not heard, but he soon became so curious that he wrote a letter to the Azusa Church, asking how he could receive the same blessing the people there had received from God. They wrote back promising to pray for him and simply advised him to tarry and to seek the baptism of the Spirit daily.

The following is Barratt's testimony of receiving the baptism in the Holy Spirit in New York City in November of 1906. Note that Barratt, who had studied voice under the famous Norwegian composer Edvard Grieg, sang beautifully in tongues.

There were not many people at the evening meeting, but God's power was mightily manifested. I asked the leader of the meeting, a little before twelve o'clock, to lay hands on me and pray for me. Immediately the power of God began to work in my body, as well as in my spirit.

I was like Daniel, powerless under the Divine touch (Dn 10:8) and had to lean upon the table on the platform, where I was sitting, and slid down on to the floor. Again my speaking organs began to move, but there was no voice to be heard. I asked a brother, a Norwegian, who had often heard me preach in Christiana, and the doctor's wife, to pray for me once more.

"Try to speak," the Norwegian said, but I answered that "if the Lord could speak through a human being, he must make me do so by his Spirit! There was to be no humbug about this!"

When they were praying, the doctor's wife saw a crown of fire over my head and a cloven tongue as of fire in front of the crown. (Compare Acts 2:3-4.) The brother from Norway, and others, saw this supernatural highly red light.

The very same moment, my being was filled with light and an

18

indescribable power, and I began to speak in a foreign language as loudly as I could. For a long time I was lying upon my back on the floor, speaking—afterwards I was moving about on my knees with my eyes shut. For some time this went on; then at last I sat on a chair, and the whole time I spoke in "diverse kinds of tongues" (1 Cor 12:10) with a short interval between.

When speaking some of these languages, there was an aching in my vocal cords. I am sure that I spoke seven or eight different languages. They were clear and plain; and the different positions of the tongue, and the different tones of the voice, and the different accents, made me understand how different the languages were, one from the other. (Now, while I am writing this the Spirit works on my vocal cords and I have to sing).

The most beautiful of all was the singing—when the inspiration reached its climax, I burst out in a wonderful baritone solo. I never heard the tune before, and did not understand the words, but it was a most beautiful language, so smooth and easy to pronounce. Those who were present and heard the whole thing, said that my voice was quite changed.

I shall never forget how beautiful and pure the singing sounded. It seemed to me the rhythm in the verses and chorus was as perfect as it is possible to be. Several times after that I sang songs, and today the Spirit has been constantly singing through me in a foreign language. I have recited poem after poem, that were given me instantaneously by the Spirit.

Now I am asking the Lord to give me the interpretation of the languages I speak.

This lasted till about four o'clock in the morning. There were nine persons present until 3 A.M., who can testify to the truth of every word I have written; some of them stayed till 4 A.M.

That experience forever lit a fire in Barratt's soul, and he made it his life mission to carry the fires of Pentecost all over the world. Upon his return to Norway, he started his periodical, *Korsets Seier*, which was eventually published in Norwegian, Swedish, Finnish, Russian, German, and Spanish. Through his periodicals, books, and travels, Thomas Barratt was instrumental in spreading pentecostalism all over Scandinavia, Europe, and in many places throughout the Third World as well.

∾

Frank Bartleman

"We belong to the whole body of Christ, both in heaven and on earth."

Frank Bartleman (1871–1935) was the most important eyewitness of the Azusa Street revival, which he chronicled in many articles to the Holiness movement periodicals of his day. His hundreds of articles on Azusa Street, many of which were published in the *Way of Faith* in Columbia, South Carolina, helped spread the word about Azusa Street to the world.

Bartleman was born in Pennsylvania and attended Temple College and Moody Bible Institute before entering the ministry. Always involved in rescue missions work among the needy, including alcoholics and prostitutes, Bartleman allied himself with the Holiness movement. He served in the Salvation Army, the Wesleyan Methodist Church, the Pillar of

Fire, and the Peniel Mission before becoming a pentecostal. Living on the edge of poverty, Bartleman worked his way to California in 1904, where he wound up working with Holiness rescue missions in Los Angeles.

By 1905 he became involved in correspondence with Evan Roberts in Wales, hoping to see a Welsh-like revival break out in Los Angeles. At this time he came into contact with William J. Seymour and attended the Azusa Street services when they began in April of 1906. His reports caught the imagination of thousands of seekers who came to Azusa Street and went out to spread the pentecostal flame around the world.

The following "plea for unity" appeared at the end of his major work, *How "Pentecost" Came to Los Angeles,* which was published in 1925.

The Spirit is laboring for the unity of believers today, for the "one body," that the prayer of Jesus may be answered, "that they all may be one, that the world may believe." But the saints are ever too ready rather to serve a system or party, to contend for religious, selfish, party interests. God's people are shut up in denominational coops. Like chicks they must get their food only in these, their own coops.

"Error always leads to militant exclusion. Truth evermore stoops to wash the saints' feet." One feels even in visiting many pentecostal missions today that they do not belong there, simply because they have not lined up officially with that particular brand or variety. These things ought not to be. "By one Spirit are we all baptized into one body" (1 Cor 12:13). We should be as one family, which we are, at home in God's house anywhere.

We belong to the whole body of Christ, both in heaven and on earth. God's church is one. It is a terrible thing to go about dismembering the "body of Christ." How foolish and wicked the petty differences between

Christians will appear in the light of eternity.

Christ is the "issue." Not some doctrine about him. The gospel leads to him. It exalts Christ, not some particular doctrine, etc. To "know Christ" is the alpha and the omega of the Christian faith and practice.

"The church was in the beginning a community of brethren, guided by a few of the brethren" (D'Aubigne). "One is your Master, even Christ; and all ye are brethren" (Mt 23:8). We have too much "leadership" spirit. These divide the "body," separate the saints.

We are coming around the circle, from the early church's fall, back to primitive love and unity, in the "one body" of Christ. This is doubtless the church for which Christ is coming, "without spot or wrinkle, or any such thing."

ॐ

Dennis Bennett

"As I spoke on I had a vivid mental picture of Jesus on the cross."

Dennis Bennett (1917–91) was born in England, the son of a Congregational minister. In 1927 the family migrated to the United States. Dennis then followed in his father's footsteps and in 1949 was ordained in the Congregational Church. After serving several Congregational parishes in America, he was ordained in the Episcopal Church and was appointed to St. Mark's Episcopal Church in Van Nuys, California in 1953.

Observing several "neo-pentecostal" believers in his church, he became more interested in the Holy Spirit. After experiencing tongues in 1959, he shocked his congregation when on a Sunday morning he announced that he had been baptized in the Holy Spirit and had spoken in tongues. His announcement is now designated as the start of the charismatic movement, in which the mainline churches and denominations also began to experience a deeper move of the Holy Spirit.

In his autobiographical book *Nine O'clock in the Morning* (1970), Bennett recounts his rather awkward and yet exciting experience when he first encountered the baptism in the Holy Spirit.

I suppose I must have prayed out loud for about twenty minutes—at least it seemed to be a long time—and was just about to give up when a very strange thing happened. My tongue tripped, just as it might when you are trying to recite a tongue twister, and I began to speak in a new language!

Right away I recognized several things: first, it wasn't some kind of psychological trick or compulsion. There was nothing compulsive about it ... it was a new language, not some kind of "baby talk." It had grammar and syntax; it had inflection and expression—and it was rather beautiful....

I was speaking the Holy Spirit's words, not mine, but I was speaking them because I chose to, and in the manner I chose. I still felt nothing out of the ordinary; no great spiritual inspiration, no special warmth of God's presence. It was interesting though and somehow refreshing, and so I spoke on for several minutes. I was about to stop.

But John said: "Don't stop. Go on. Go on speaking."

It proved to be good advice. I went on, allowing the new words to come to my lips, and after three or four more minutes began to sense something new. This language was being given me from the central place in me where God was, far beyond the realm of my emotions.

Speaking on and on, I became more and more aware of God in me. The words didn't mean anything to me as language, but God knew exactly what they meant. God living in me was creating the language.

I was speaking it—giving it voice, by my volition, and I was speaking it to God who was above and beyond me. God the Holy Spirit was giving me the words to talk to God the Father, and it was all happening because of God the Son, Jesus Christ. As I spoke on I had a vivid mental picture of Jesus on the cross.

∾

Reinhard Bonnke

"Jesus Christ, the spotless, the perfect Lamb of God. He came to save sinners!"

Reinhard Willi Gottfried Bonnke (1940–) was born in Königsburg, Germany, in the home of a pentecostal pastor. Educated in Wales, he met George Jeffries and was inspired to follow his example as a healing evangelist. Later he felt called to be a missionary to Africa and arrived in Lesotho in 1964. He was sent by the German Federation of Free Pentecostal Churches (BFP).

In 1975, after mediocre success as a traditional missionary, Bonnke held his first mass healing crusade in Gaberones, Botswana. The crusade began with only a hundred persons the first night, but ended with 10,000 persons packing a local stadium. By 1983, after overfilling a tent seating 10,000 persons, he bought the largest evangelistic tent in history, which seated more than 34,000 persons.

Even this tent soon proved to be too small for the multitudes that pressed in to see the signs and wonders that occurred in his meetings. As word spread about sensational healings, Bonnke's fame spread throughout Africa. His theme in these meetings was "Africa shall be saved." In each crusade he held "fire conferences" to rally thousands of local pastors to support his meetings.

The blue-eyed German evangelist was at a loss to understand his mass appeal to the Africans. Nevertheless, his meetings grew to such enormous size that he abandoned the tent and moved to open air meetings in large fields. In time, crowds of 500,000 grew to over 1,000,000 in some services.

The climactic meeting of his ministry came in November 2000 in the "Millennium Crusade" in Lagos, Nigeria, when more than 10,000,000 persons attended the weeklong gathering. On the last night, more than 2,000,000 were in attendance, and a long-standing prophecy was fulfilled when more than 1,000,000 converts signed cards accepting Christ as their personal Savior. By 2000, Bonnke had preached to the largest single gatherings in the history of Christian evangelism. Here is his account of the final service in the fields outside the city of Lagos.

Dear friends, there are times in life when you just stand in awe of what God is doing by his Holy Spirit, right in front of your very eyes. Our millennium crusade in Lagos, Nigeria, turned out to be one of these experiences for me. I received a prophecy many years ago that I would one day see a million souls saved in a single service; and on the final night this came to pass. The decision card count on that day was l,093,745. The testimonies of salvation, deliverance, and miraculous healings were too numerous to count.

Throughout the week we received a total of 3.4 million decision cards; to God be the glory. We also held our Fire Conference for pastors and church workers in the national stadium, and over eighty thousand gathered to receive their flame of fire in order to go out and effectively fulfill the great commission. Jesus does not call us because of what we are, but because of what he makes from us. Jesus chose ordinary people, people like me and people like you.

The following is a healing testimony of a young man who produced hospital documents proving that his former condition of tuberculosis was now negative:

As I began to pray I believed that God above would move down to where I had these specimens and cause them to be negative. When Bonnke said, "Be healed from tuberculosis in the name of Jesus," I believed God. So he prayed and then he said, "Tuberculosis be healed in Jesus name," so I said, "Amen, case dismissed."

The following is a salvation testimony from a young man who signed a conversion card.

I was a sinner; I used to go to church, but I had not submitted my life to Christ. But when I came to the crusade yesterday, when he was preaching, I was saved by the blood of Jesus, by the power of the blood of Jesus. And from my desperation he touched me. I give my life to Christ. Now he is my personal Savior.

William Branham

"You will preach to multitudes the world over."

William Marrion Branham (1909–65) was born in a log cabin in Kentucky with little opportunity for education. From his youth, he was a mystic who believed that angels personally spoke to him about his future ministry. Beginning as an independent Missionary Baptist preacher, he joined the Oneness Pentecostals in 1937 after establishing a church in Jeffersonville, Indiana, known as "Branham Tabernacle." In 1946 Branham reported that an angel with black hair and a deep voice first appeared to him, and at later times the same angel gave him prophetic directions for his life and ministry.

By 1947 Branham was attracting large crowds to his services and bringing renewed attention to public healing services, which had waned after the death of Aimee Semple McPherson in 1944. People thronged to his meetings not only to witness healing miracles, but to hear him give personal information to apparent strangers through "words of knowledge."

By 1948 a whole wave of healing evangelists began to emerge, leading mass healing crusades across America and the world. Among these were Oral Roberts, Jack Coe, and A. A. Allen. Branham had a profound influence on these and other healing evangelists that followed. He died in 1965 in an automobile accident.

In the following excerpts, Branham described the messages he received in three angelic appearances that helped launch his ministry. The angel told him:

Don't ever drink, or smoke, or defile your body in any way. There will be a work for you to do when you get older.

As John the Baptist foreran the first coming of Jesus Christ, so you will forerun his second coming.

Fear not, I am sent from the presence of Almighty God to tell you that your peculiar birth and misunderstood life have been to indicate that you are to take a gift of divine healing to the peoples of the world. If you will be sincere when you pray, and can get the people to believe you, nothing shall stand before your prayer, not even cancer. You will go into many parts of the earth and will pray for kings and rulers and potentates. You will preach to multitudes the world over and thousands will come to you for counsel. You must tell them that their thoughts speak louder in heaven than their words.

As the prophet Moses was given two signs to prove he was sent from God, so you will be given two signs. First: when you take a person's right hand in your left hand, you will be able to detect the presence of any germ-caused disease by vibrations that will appear in your left hand. Then you must pray for the person. If your hand returns to normal, you can pronounce the person healed; if it doesn't, just ask a blessing and walk away.

Under the anointing from God, do not try to think your own thoughts; it will come to pass that you will be able to tell by vision the very secrets of their hearts. Then the people will have to believe you. This will initiate the gospel in power that will bring on the second coming of Christ.

The following is an account of Branham's first recorded miracle, which occurred in 1946.

Soon afterwards his first miracle occurred when Margie Morgan, a church member in Jeffersonville, was brought unconscious to him for prayer. In the last stages of cancer, the doctors had given up on hopes for her recovery. When Branham prayed for her "his wrist and lower arm tingled fiercely, just as if he had touched a mild electrical current. Vibrations moved up his arm all the way to his heart. His wristwatch stopped....

"When he asked Jesus Christ to heal this dying woman, the vibrations stopped ... now the demon was gone." Branham then declared, "Sir, don't fear; for thus saith the Lord, 'Your wife will live!'" Her recovery was so complete that her doctor released her from the hospital a short time later.

Harald Bredesen

"It was just as if a bottle was uncorked."

Harald Bredesen (1918–) was ordained as a Lutheran minister in 1944. As a young man he was dissatisfied with his Christian life and ministry. He became concerned with the disconnect between the passion and power of the early New Testament church portrayed in the Book of Acts as compared to his own life and ministry. He began diligently to study the Scriptures in an attempt to discover what was the secret of the early church.

The young pastor became convinced that the secret was the power of the Holy Spirit that the early believers possessed. In 1946 he was baptized in the Holy Spirit and spoke in tongues in the Glad Tidings Assemblies of God Church in downtown Manhattan.

Bredesen was used to help introduce many others to the fullness of the Spirit. He also worked with Catholics to help bring renewal to the Catholic Church as well. Among the well-known men who were influenced by him were Pat Boone, John Sherrill, and Pat Robertson. Bredesen even helped coin the term "charismatic renewal," which has now spread across the globe.

The following testimony of Bredesen's baptism in the Holy Spirit is given in his 1982 autobiography *Yes, Lord.*

Up to this point, I had wanted power for service, power for witness, and power to live the Christian life. Now I had one desire, and that was to satisfy the yearning heart of Jesus with myself. Previously I had loved God with reservation, had served him with reservation, and therefore I had assumed that he loved me—with reservation.

In that moment it seemed as if all my sins and repeated failures and shortcomings had no more power to shut out his love for me than a fly-speck could shut out the sun. In spite of what I was, in spite of what I was not, in spite of all my reservations, he loved me without reservation. I was so overwhelmed, overjoyed, and amazed by the total unreservedness of his love for me that my hands went up in awe. Now I didn't have to ask anybody, "Why do you raise your hands?" It was just involuntary wonder and surrender.

I tried to say, "Thank you, Jesus, thank you, Jesus," but I couldn't express the inexpressible. Then, to my great relief, the Holy Spirit did it for me. It was just as if a bottle was uncorked, and out of me poured a torrent of words in a language I had never studied before. Now everything I had ever wanted to say to God, I could say.

After a long time of praising God and knowing that this experience was real came the return of the realization that I was going to have to tell my friends. I knew what they would say: "Harald, you have gotten yourself mixed up with a group of hysterical people who whip themselves up into a frenzy of religious excitement and then let off steam in a form of ecstatic gibberish. All this has rubbed off on you."

I prayed, "Lord, if this is a true language, then you can reveal it to me." I went out the door and down one of the many paths that lead into the surrounding woods. As I walked along this path, my new prayer tongue was flowing, an artesian spring within me, of praise and adoration.

Coming up the path was a pretty, flaxen-haired girl of about eleven. When she came to me, she stood and cocked her head and then laughed. "You're speaking Polish."

I wrote on a slip of paper, "Where is there a Polish man? I want to speak to him." I was afraid to start speaking in English, for fear I'd never be able to begin again in this tongue. The girl led me to a man who was standing on the front steps of his cabin; he was squat and muscular, maybe a Pennsylvania miner. I thought, "Just think, I've never met this man, but in Christ we are brothers."

He exclaimed, "Bracia, Bracia! You call me Brother." He said, "You are praising God, going from one Slavic dialect to the other."

When I left him, my heart was overjoyed.

∾

J.W. Buckalew

"Gambling houses, poolrooms, and church ice cream suppers were closed out."

J.W. Buckalew was a legendary preacher in the early history of the pentecostal revival. Beginning in the Pentecostal Holiness Church, he soon joined the Church of God headquartered in Cleveland, Tennessee. His was a rough-and-tumble ministry reminiscent of the early American Methodist preacher Peter Cartwright.

Like many early preachers in the Holiness-Pentecostal churches, Buckalew was a fighter of sin and those powers behind the sin industry, especially liquor dealers, pimps, and prostitutes. He spent many nights in jail after antagonizing law enforcement powers of the Southern cities where he put up his tent. Often challenged, he was not averse to ending disputes with his fists.

The following testimony is an account of a revival in Alabama City, Alabama, in September 1910 as reported in the October 15 edition of the *Church of God and Evening Light Evangel*, the official paper of the Church of God edited by A.J. Tomlinson. Certainly no one could ignore the pentecostals when they came to town.

The meeting closed in Alabama City, September 25. It was one of the greatest meetings of our lives. We preached to thousands of people standing around a little gospel tent.

Gambling houses, poolrooms, and church ice cream suppers were closed out. We kept a record of those that were saved and baptized with the Holy Ghost, until they came through in such large numbers that we just quit trying. Something over one hundred got the baptism.

The Holy Ghost was there in such great power that sometimes we went into the pulpit to preach and saw the power on the people, so then we laid down our Bibles and began to invite them to the altar. Sometimes over a hundred hungry souls would make a rush to the altar and begin crying through to God. This sight I shall never forget.

This stirred the devil, and many times the devil's crowd invited us to leave the town, or they would burn the tent; but wife and I and a few faithful young men stayed and guarded the tent and defeated their plans until the Board of Aldermen and Mayor of the city wrote to Cleveland, Tennessee, to find out how they got rid of the "holiness people." The answer stated that they just put them in jail and burned their tent. So last Friday night at eleven o'clock while Sister Buckalew, Brother Grayham, Brother McMertry, and I were eating a lunch, three drunken officers came up and demanded our arrest, to which we submitted quietly.

They marched us out from under our tent and up to the street to the stone jail, where they brutally threw us in like murderers. Glory to God! When the huge lock clicked and had taken the freedom from J.W. Buckalew, Hubert McMertry, and J.H. Grayham, we began to shout. Sister Buckalew was permitted to stay with the wife of the turnkey.

All night long we prayed and sang and shouted. Immediately they left the jail and returned to the tent, cut it down, and set fire to it. While the flames were ascending we were in the iron cells praising God that we were counted worthy to suffer shame for his sake.

Morning dawned; the sun with its golden rays peeped from behind the eastern horizon and found its way down upon a stone jail. The people began to arise. Hush! Listen! was exclaimed. They heard the shouting and singing of Buckalew, Grayham, McMertry, and Sister Buckalew.

A crowd began to gather outside. I heard the sighs and sobs of broken hearts. The crowd continued to gather. Outside I saw my sisters weeping. The crowd continued to gather and at eight o'clock we sang, "Jesus Passed This Way Before."

Then we called them to prayer. Such a sight I never saw before. Men and women were on their faces or under the power of God.

Nine o'clock came. We heard the huge lock click and we were commanded to come out; then they marched us up into the large hall. Here they told us that if we would comply with their rules we could go free. We did not promise to do anything but to go back and preach. Then they gave us unconditional freedom.

Saturday night came. We had straightened up the remains of a little gospel tent; by dark a thousand had gathered. By 7:30, two thousand had gathered—an acre of humanity—men, women, and children. We preached to them from the text in Acts 4:29. Eternity alone will tell the effect of this meeting.

We had the pleasure of baptizing fifty-nine in this meeting. Some more are to be baptized yet.

We are here at Armuchee, Georgia; the meeting commenced last night. We will be here fifteen days. Pray for us here.

Yours in the battle till Jesus comes, J.W. Buckalew and wife.

❦

Howard Carter

"A definite experience of boundless love and joy filled me."

Alfred Howard Carter (1891–1981) was born in Aston, Birmingham, England. Carter was a great artist. As a boy he loved to draw. At age twelve his work was already being displayed in London's Gallery of Art.

When he was saved at age twenty, he struggled between his art and the call of God to ministry that he felt on his life. He eventually submitted himself to God's call. At this time he joined a local Church of Christ. After his initial service to God he found out about a deeper experience available to all who sought it. He and his brother John began earnestly to seek the baptism of the Spirit.

After his pentecostal experience, Carter became a founding member of the British Assemblies of God in 1924. Afterwards he served with distinction as an editor, educator, and leader in several World Pentecostal Conferences.

The following is his testimony of receiving the baptism in the Holy Spirit in 1915.

Howard and John were both earnestly seeking the Pentecostal experience. Although many prayed for them (at the Sunderland Whitsuntide Conventions in 1913 and 1914, for example, hands were laid upon them), they did not receive their personal Pentecost. In

1915 Howard and John cycled down from Birmingham to a pente-costal convention in Bedford under the chairmanship of Pastor Robert Anderson Jardine.

When the opening hymn was being sung, Howard got down on his knees to pray. Soon he was praying and praising in such a loud voice that he was disturbing the meeting; Mr. Jardine asked his church elder to lead "the noisy brother into the vestry." Once in there he burst out in tongues and warmly embraced the elder in an ecstasy of joy. Previously Howard had not accepted that tongues were essential and had keenly opposed a leader who had taught that speaking in tongues was the ini-ial physical evidence of the baptism in the Spirit. His testimony now hanged:

"The power of the Spirit flooded my being and I broke forth in other mgues for the first time in my experience.... A definite experience of boundless love and joy filled me, a joy I cannot express, a joy unspeak-ible and full of glory, for I felt like singing and praising God contin-ually. Moreover the cross of Calvary seemed so wonderfully great to me and the atonement so much more wonderful than ever before. A deep consciousness of the abiding presence of the Lord was blessedly mine from that hour."

After this experience, Carter tried unsuccessfully to share his new pentecostal experience with his local Church of Christ congregation in Sparkbrook. According to their testimony, the church refused to accept his testimony and he was put out of the church.

∾

G.B. Cashwell

"Came 3,000 miles for his Pentecost."

Gaston Barnabas Cashwell (1862–1916) has often been called the "Apostle of Pentecost to the South" because of his barnstorming ministry in the Southeast in 1907, which resulted in the conversion of many Holiness churches to the new pentecostal movement. Born in 1862 in Sampson County, North Carolina, Cashwell was ordained in the Methodist Episcopal Church, South and was an aspiring young Methodist preacher when he came under the influence of A.B. Crumpler, founder of the infant Pentecostal Holiness Church. After joining the church in 1903, he heard about the Pentecostal outpouring at the Azusa Street Mission in Los Angeles. Following much prayer, his wife agreed that he should travel to Los Angeles to seek for the pentecostal blessing.

In November 1906 he visited the Azusa Street Mission, which was led by the black Holiness preacher William J. Seymour. At first repelled by the services, Cashwell later became a full seeker for the pentecostal experience. After receiving the gift of tongues, he returned to North Carolina, where he led a historic meeting in January 1907 that attracted multitudes of seekers. Within the next six months, he served as the catalyst for at least five Holiness groups' becoming part of the exploding pentecostal movement in the South. Later his paper, *The Bridegroom's Messenger,* became a major force in consolidating his pioneering pentecostal work in the South.

Cashwell's testimony was published in Seymour's *Apostolic Faith* newspaper, which was published from Azusa Street.

About two months ago, I began to read in the Way of Faith *the reports of the meetings in Azusa Mission, Los Angeles. I had been preaching holiness for nine years, but my soul began to hunger and thirst for the fullness of God. The Spirit led me more and more to seek Pentecost.*

After praying and weeping before God for many days, he put it into my heart to go to Los Angeles to seek the baptism with the Holy Ghost. My wife prayed and went with me till we both got the witness that it was the will of God for me to go. The devil fought me and laid the hand of affliction on my wife and I felt it almost impossible for me to come.

The night I left home, wife and I prayed and wept before the Lord and God gave the victory, and we both consented on our knees that if we died we would be in the order of the Lord and that God would take us home. I immediately rose and took my valise in hand, went to the depot, and started for Los Angeles. Glory to God.

I was six days on the road, was fasting and praying to the Lord continually. As soon as I reached Azusa Mission, a new crucifixion began in my life and I had to die to many things, but God gave me the victory.

The first altar call I went forward earnest for my Pentecost. I struggled from Sunday till Thursday. While seeking in an upstairs room in the mission, the Lord opened up the windows of heaven and the light of God began to flow over me in such power as never before.

I then went into the room where the service was held, and Sister Lum was reading of how the Holy Ghost was falling in other places. Before I knew it, I began to speak in tongues and praise God. A brother interpreted some of the words to be "I love God with all my soul."

He filled me with his Spirit and love, and I am now feasting and drinking at the fountain continually and speak as the Spirit gives utterance both in my own language and in the unknown language. I find that all has to be surrendered to God, our own language and all, and he speaks through us English, German, Greek or any other tongue in his own will and way.

The Lord also healed my body. I had been afflicted with rheumatism for years, and at a healing service held here, I was anointed and prayed for and was immediately healed of rheumatism and catarrh and have a sound body and clothed in my right mind.

Oswald Chambers

"Have you had your Pentecost yet?"

Oswald Chambers (1874–1917) was born in Aberdeen, Scotland. He was converted to Christ under the ministry of the celebrated British preacher Charles Spurgeon. Feeling God's call to a teaching ministry, Chambers prepared himself at Dunoon College, where he studied theology. He was soon teaching across the globe in the United States, Europe, Asia, and Africa. In time he became associated with the Holiness movement, and for a short time was a teacher at Martin Wells Knapp's God's Bible School in Cincinnati, Ohio. He was a prolific writer and evangelist.

Although not known as a pentecostal, Chambers was very much aware of the Christian's need for being filled with the Holy Spirit in order to carry out one's life calling. He equated the baptism in the Holy Spirit with entire sanctification, as did many of the "Higher Life" leaders associated with the Keswick conventions in England. Today some scholars would refer to him as a "pre-pentecostal."

Though he passed away almost one hundred years ago, his spiritual devotionals are still as powerful today as when they were first published in 1935. His great work, *My Utmost for His Highest*, has become a Christian classic. It has been continuously in print for over sixty-five years.

The following is Chambers' own account of his dramatic personal Pentecost.

The only holiness there is, is the holiness of God. The gospel is not that God loves me with unmerited mercy and blots out my sins. It is that God not only does that, but enables me to love others with a love like his; enables me to show unmerited mercy like he showed me. The miracle of what Jesus Christ came to do is in making characters stamped and sealed by Golgotha and Pentecost.

Have you had your Pentecost yet?

Don't say you think you have. Does any man think that he is married? A man and a woman when married know it, and can tell the day that they were. A man who is baptized with the Holy Ghost knows the very moment, the very place, the very spot the transaction was done; and he will never forget it.

I remember the place. An old wooden pew in the west of Scotland, in a Baptist Church; and that is so photographed in my mind that I will never forget it through time and eternity. O bless God! That is not slipping into anything. It is a definite, personal Pentecost, and unless

40

you have had a definite, personal Pentecost, you are suffering from a legal fiction. You are trying to reckon you are sanctified and you are not. When you are sanctified you will not reckon it.

Go down before him. And let him do a definite work.

∾

Florence Crawford

"The power of God shook my being, and rivers of joy and divine love flooded my soul. Oh, it was wonderful!"

Florence Louise Crawford (1872–1936) was born in the home of an atheist and was afflicted as a child with spinal meningitis with resulting poor eyesight. In 1906, after an evangelical conversion, she happened to hear about the Azusa Street Mission and attended services conducted by Pastor William J. Seymour. In a short time she received an experience of sanctification, baptism in the Holy Spirit attested to by speaking in tongues, and complete healing of her afflictions. Despite these experiences, her husband refused to accept the pentecostal movement until after her death.

In a short time, Crawford became a leading member of the Azusa Street staff, helping Seymour in editing the paper *Apostolic Faith*. In 1909, she left Los Angeles and founded the Apostolic Faith Mission in Portland, Oregon. Many believe that she left after opposing Seymour's marriage to Jenny Moore. At any rate, she took the mailing list for Seymour's

Apostolic Faith paper with her and continued its publication from Portland.

Crawford went on to found her own Holiness-Pentecostal denomination with the name "Apostolic Faith." Although this group remained small in the United States, it founded flourishing mission churches overseas.

The following is her testimony of her baptism in the Holy Spirit at Azusa Street in 1906.

How I thank God that when I heard of the latter outpouring of the Holy Ghost, he led me to that little mission. It was not a fine hall, just an old barn-like building with only an old board laid on two chairs for an altar. The floor was carpeted with sawdust; the walls and beams blackened by smoke.

I looked around to see if anybody saw me go in, but I would not have cared if the whole world saw me go out. I had found a people that had the experience I wanted. The first "hallelujah" I heard echoed down in my soul. When I went out of there that day I felt so little. The only thing I wondered was, can I ever get it?

From Monday morning till Friday at four o'clock, I lay on my face, between my duties (you can do your work and do it well and seek God, too). I lay on my face and shed tears and read my Bible. That Friday afternoon at the mission, the preacher stopped and said, "Somebody in this place wants something from God." I pushed the chairs away in front of me and fell at the altar. And the fire fell and God sanctified me. The power of God went through me like thousands of needles.

"He sanctified me" were the only words I could speak for days after the fire fell on my heart. If you get the real experience you will never deny it. It will stand when you face all hell. It can weather any storm.

Three days later, after living with Jesus alone, a great hunger seized me and down I went before God. He showed me I must be baptized with the Holy Ghost and fire. He showed me that the temple was clean, that the Holy Ghost could come only on clean vessels.

And how I pled with him and prayed and praised God and consecrated! Yes, I consecrated again, deeper and deeper, and sought for the power to tell the world what great things God had done for me. I sought till the following Friday.

As I sat in my chair in the mission, the Holy Ghost fell from heaven and a rushing mighty wind filled the room. This tongue that never spoke another word but English began to magnify and praise God in another language. I was speaking in Chinese, and it was the sweetest thing I ever heard in my life.

The power of God shook my being, and rivers of joy and divine love flooded my soul. Oh, it was wonderful! But the greatest joy to my heart was that I had received the power to witness to lost souls that they might find Jesus.

I was a wreck in my body, but I never once thought of the healing of my body until God baptized me with the Holy Ghost and fire. I had worn glasses for years. Three attacks of spinal meningitis early in my life had left my head and eyes so affected that I could not leave the glasses off. I went to the mission that afternoon and told what wonderful things the Lord had done for me, and had them pray, and the healing power of the Son of God flowed through my eyes, and my eyes were perfect.

∿

Gerald Derstine

"It gushed uncontrollably from the depths of my being like a geyser."

Gerald Derstine (1928–) was born the second of three children to Pennsylvanian Mennonites. He was reared in a very strict manner and his family belonged to the more conservative stream of the Mennonite faith. In 1949 he had heard about the dynamic preaching and healings that were occurring in pentecostal meetings, so he attended one out of curiosity.

It was in this meeting, conducted by evangelist T. L. Osborn, that Gerald and his wife, Beulah, felt conviction of sin and gave their hearts to Christ. Hearing from the evangelist that God can heal if people will confess his Word, he began claiming healing for the extreme stuttering that had plagued him for twenty years. Six weeks later he was completely delivered of the condition.

Derstine later felt God's call to ministry and in 1953 was named pastor of the Strawberry Lake Mennonite Church in Minnesota. Feeling an intense burden for the community, Gerald and his associate pastor prayed together every morning and fasted weekly for the church and the local people. One year later a mighty revival broke out in his conservative Mennonite church.

After a group of fourteen teenagers received Christ, the

whole church broke out into revival. People began to be slain in the Spirit, prophesy, and speak with tongues. A few days later Gerald had his own pentecostal experience. It was in his bedroom late at night when the Spirit moved.

"Gerald, do you remember the prophecy which said that before you spoke in tongues you would have to go through a hard battle?"

I nodded. "Yes, I remember." So this was it!

"Gerald, this was not Mr. Carlton you were facing. That was his body you saw and his voice you heard, but Satan was in his body. Gerald, you showed your love to Mr. Carlton. Therefore, reach out and take hold of my hand."

Joy was standing on the opposite side of the bed. Beulah still was in the bed and Amos stood next to Joy. I hesitated momentarily before taking her hand. It bothered me that she'd said I had shown my love to Mr. Carlton. It wasn't my love. I could never have loved that man in that condition. No way. It had to be a supernatural love—one that came straight from God. I couldn't take credit for it.

Nevertheless, I reached out in the semi-darkness and clasped Joy's hand.

The moment I touched her hand I burst forth like a mighty fountain that had just been unplugged—in a language I had never learned. It gushed uncontrollably from the depths of my being like a geyser. At first it seemed as if I were rebuking the devil. Then an overwhelming joy came over me and I literally trembled from head to foot out of sheer exuberance.

The trembling was so intense that I nearly danced all over that bedroom. My tongue was going a mile a minute, and all I could feel was unspeakable joy and gratitude, praise and love for Jesus. I never wanted to stop. This had to be heaven—forever and ever praising him, enjoying a high that just kept increasing in intensity!

But after I had gone on in this manner for a time, I dimly heard Amos's voice commanding me to stop.

"Gerald, stop! In the name of Jesus, stop!"

How could he do this to me? I didn't want to stop and furthermore, I didn't think I could if I wanted to. With great effort, however, I obeyed and finally got my body and tongue under control.

Then Amos interpreted in English all that I had said in tongues. And as soon as his interpretation was finished, he and Joy left the room and climbed the stairs back to their bedrooms. The first hint of dawn had diluted the darkness when I crawled back into bed, still feeling like I was in another world.

∽

John Alexander Dowie

"Death hovered hungrily over its expected victim."

John Alexander Dowie (1847–1907) was born in Edinburgh, Scotland. He was very sickly as a child, so much so that he could not even finish school. In 1867 his family migrated to Australia.

Dowie was self-educated and had a great love for books. He had read the Bible completely through by age six. He gave his heart to Christ as a small child, but still continued to be plagued by frequent illnesses.

Although at the time divine healing was not a popular theology, Dowie became convinced from the Scriptures that God desires to heal the whole person—body, soul, and spirit. As a young man at the time, he was suffering from chronic dyspepsia. He cried out to God and was completely healed. This started his journey and desire to see others healed as well.

Ordained in the Australian Congregational Church after studies in Edinburgh University in Scotland, Dowie pastored several churches before beginning a healing ministry in 1878. This work led him to the United States in 1888, where he soon became famous for his healing services. In 1893 he gained notoriety after setting up a healing tabernacle at the Chicago World's Fair.

In the late 1890s Dowie established Zion City, Illinois, where he published *Leaves of Healing* magazine and established the Christian Catholic Church. His Zion tabernacle seated no less than 8,000 persons.

Among the notable healings claimed through his ministry was one that occurred in the life of President Abraham Lincoln's cousin, Miss Amanda M. Hicks. The following is Dowie's account of Amanda Hicks' healing.

Carried four hundred miles on a bed, in intense agony, and healed in a moment, was the story of the healing of Amanda Hicks, cousin to President Abraham Lincoln. She was carried from her home in Clinton, Kentucky, where for a number of years she had been President of Clinton College. The cot was made by one of her pupils, after measuring the width of the door of a Pullman sleeping car, so that she might be carried in and transferred to bed, since she could not be lifted.

Weeping, and fearing that they should see her face no more, her scholars and friends bade her a sad farewell. On January 30, she reached Chicago, and was brought in an ambulance to a room on Ellis Avenue. Her companion, leaving at once to inquire for Dr. Dowie, and locating him, told how Miss Hicks had suffered paroxysms of pain, for long months, night and day, and had been only temporarily relieved by large doses of morphine.

Physicians failed to diagnose the case, saying it was "wrapped in mystery." The lady further explained that they had been impressed to come to Dr. Dowie, after a young student, very skeptical concerning the miracles of the Bible, had come to Chicago to investigate divine healing and was so impressed that he returned to Clinton, Kentucky, and stood by the sick woman's bedside urging her to come. Miss Hicks, after carefully reading her Bible, was convinced of God's way of healing and as a result had come to Chicago.

The first thing that Dr. Dowie did was to demand that she give up morphine and drugs at once. It was a terrific battle; Dr. Dowie and his wife visited her from time to time, from mid-afternoon until midnight, fighting against the terrible power of the morphine drug. Dr. Dowie describes the battle in the following words:

"We saw that she must be removed to our home, if we were to help her effectually, and to be used of God in the healing. The case was one of the gravest and most immediate peril. Death hovered hungrily over its expected victim, and Satan hoped to destroy a noble and useful life, which longed only to live for Christ and humanity. Therefore, we took the risk of having her removed on a bitterly cold day, with the frozen snow lying deeply on the ground.

"But disease was to be the victim and Christ was to be the Victor in the fight. That day, we prayed, and laid our hands upon her in the name of Jesus. In a moment, the terrible agony of months departed, and later in the evening she rose and walked freely. Several days of cleansing followed, gallons of cancerous matter passing away, and she was reduced by six inches in circumference. Strength came quickly, good appetite, good food, and above all the infinitely good God, gave her power to go out and to walk even in the snow."

✑

David du Plessis

"Oh, Lord," I said, "please don't send me to China."

No one had more lasting influence on the pentecostal/charismatic movement in the last half of the twentieth century than David Johannes du Plessis (1905–87). He was born in a town called Twenty-Four Rivers in South Africa. His father was a lay pentecostal preacher who came into the pentecostal movement under the influence of John G. Lake.

Young David was converted in 1916 and was baptized in the Holy Spirit in 1918. Afterwards, he was ordained in the Apostolic Faith Mission church (AFM), the largest pentecostal denomination in South Africa. He rose to leadership in the church and in the world pentecostal movement before immigrating to the United States in 1947. During this period, he served as an organizing secretary for the World Pentecostal Conference and as a visionary leader in founding the Pentecostal Fellowship of North America (PFNA).

In the 1950s du Plessis became the first pentecostal to dialogue with the World Council of Churches (WCC), thus raising opposition from the American pentecostal churches. In 1962 he surrendered his ordination by the Assemblies of God under pressure and became an ambassador without portfolio, speaking for the pentecostals in many ecumenical venues. In this period, he attended six international sessions of the

World Council of Churches and was invited as a pentecostal observer to the sessions of Vatican II from 1963 to 1965.

When the charismatic movement entered the mainline churches in force after 1960, du Plessis entered on a worldwide itinerary of meetings with almost every stream of it in the world. Before his death in 1987, du Plessis had been reinstated in the Assemblies of God and was widely called "Mr. Pentecost."

The following is the account of du Plessis' baptism in the Holy Spirit in 1918.

The joy overwhelmed me, and I said, "Hallelujah." But that was no good; it didn't express what I was feeling. "Praise the Lord" was no better. It sounded silly in comparison with the sheer joy surging through me.

"How can I express it?" I thought. But before I could go any further, I began to laugh. And I laughed, on and on, "Ha ha ha ha, ho ho ho ho, he he he he, ha ha ha ha...." I felt I couldn't laugh any more.

Nobody stopped me. Some of them laughed a bit with me, obviously because I was laughing so hard, harder than anyone I'd ever heard. But no one seemed upset. I held my stomach and said, "Lord, I can't take it any more. Help me ... help me to release what I'm feeling," and I started to shout hallelujah again. I got as far as "ha-a-a ...," but the "lelujah" wouldn't come.

I began to speak in tongues, new sounds that I had never heard before. The "ha-a-a" had opened my mouth, and the Lord had filled it with a new language. It was a very funny language, it seemed to me.

An old sailor was in the meeting, Bob Masser, who had been around the world. He heard me speaking those strange new sounds there in the corner and walked close to me to listen for several moments. He then turned and shouted to the crowd, "David is speaking Chinese! I've heard it many times. He's praising God in pure Chinese!"

*And the people began to marvel and praise God themselves. I quick-
ly stopped speaking, with a frightening thought on my mind. "Oh,
Lord," I said, "please don't send me to China." I was afraid that was
an indication of a missionary assignment.*

*But, in a few moments, the thought vanished, and I began to speak
again, wondering whether I had lost the gift. I was immediately aware
that the language had changed. It was distinctly different, obviously
not Oriental. I kept on speaking, and my mind was whirring with all
kinds of thoughts.*

*"What language is that now?... Have I disobeyed the Spirit by
changing tongues?... Now what have I got?... It sounds like babbling.... But if it's babbling, why can't I keep up the same kind of babbling?... Who changes the babbling?... Why can't I do that first language again?... I've spoken over six different languages.... It's new
every time.... I guess I'm not doing this.... I'm speaking ... but I'm not
making the sounds.... They just keep forming on my lips ... and I can't
change them.... But I can't keep them up, either ..."*

*After nearly half an hour of this, I went over to the preacher and
said, "Brother Heatley, when the Spirit gives you the gift of tongues,
does he give you one language only and then that's your gift and you
always speak the same language?"*

*"No," he replied, "the Bible refers in First Corinthians 12 to 'diverse
kinds of tongues.' We may have many kinds. What's your problem,
anyway?"*

*"Well," I said, "I think I have spoken half a dozen languages in the
last half hour."*

"Don't worry about that," he said, chuckling.

༃

William H. Durham

"Brother Durham has got his Pentecost. Glory to God."

William H. Durham (1873–1912) was one of the most important of the early pentecostal leaders and father of the "finished work" theory of sanctification that led to the organization of the Assemblies of God in 1911. Beginning his ministry as a Baptist, Durham later became an articulate leader in the Holiness movement. In 1901 he became pastor of the North Avenue Mission in Chicago. After hearing of the Pentecostal revival at Azusa Street, he traveled to Los Angeles in 1907 to seek for the baptism in the Holy Spirit under the influence of pastor William J. Seymour.

A constant seeker at the altar, Durham finally received the coveted tongues-attested baptism on March 2, 1907. At this time, Seymour prophesied that wherever Durham preached "the Holy Ghost would fall upon the people." Indeed, in a short time hundreds of people entered the ranks of the pentecostals, not only speaking in tongues, but exhibiting a spiritual manifestation that some called "the Durham jerks."

In 1910, Durham began to teach what he called the "finished work of Calvary," which denied the "second blessing" Holiness view that had been universally held by the first pentecostals. Much of his theology may have come as a result of meetings with E. W. Kenyon, who had already taught "finished work" sanctification for several years. As a result of Durham's influence, large numbers of pentecostals abandoned the Wesleyan second blessing teaching and formed hundreds of independent pentecostal churches around the nation. In 1914, the Assemblies of God were formed by Durham's followers.

The following is Durham's testimony of his baptism in the Holy Spirit at Azusa Street.

The first thing that impressed me was the love and unity that prevailed in the meeting and the heavenly sweetness that filled the very air that I breathed. I want to say right here, that I have attended many large Holiness camp meetings and conventions, but I never felt the power and glory that I felt in Azusa Street Mission, and when about twenty persons joined in singing the "Heavenly Chorus," it was the most ravishing and unearthly music that ever fell on mortal ears....

It seemed and still seems to me, I could not sing in that chorus. I know it came direct from heaven. I at once became an earnest seeker, and day after day, I went down before the Lord and he was true to me.

He showed me myself as he saw me. I can never forget the state of utter helplessness to which he reduced me. He even took away the spirit of prayer, my testimony was removed from me, I saw myself apart from Christ as it were, and it made me desperate.

I can never forget the faithfulness of Sister Good and others in dealing with me. Next to God, I am indebted to them, dear faithful souls, laying down their lives for others; and all the reward they receive so far as I can see, was the plain clothing they wear and the food they eat.

After I had been there for a little over two weeks, devoting the entire time to seeking my Pentecost, on Tuesday afternoon, when very much disheartened, suddenly the power of God descended upon me, and I went down under it. I have no language to describe what took place, but it was wonderful. It seemed to me that my body had suddenly become porous, and that a current of electricity was being turned on me from all sides; and for two hours I lay under his mighty power, and yet I knew I was not baptized yet, though I literally felt transparent, and a wonderful glory had come into my soul. Again on Thursday evening following, his power came over me, and I was prostrate for two hours, and still I knew I was not baptized, though I received a great spiritual uplift.

But on Friday evening, March 1, his mighty power came over me, until I jerked and quaked under it for about three hours. It was strange and wonderful and yet glorious. He worked my whole body, one section at a time, first my arm, then my limbs, then my body, then my face, then my chin, and finally at 1 A.M., Saturday, March 2, after being under the power for three hours, he finished the work on my vocal organs, and spoke through me in unknown tongues.

I arose, perfectly conscious outwardly and inwardly that I was fully baptized in the Holy Ghost, and the devil can never tempt me to doubt it. First I was conscious that a living person had come into me, and that he possessed even my physical being, in a literal sense, in so much that he could as his will take hold of my vocal organs, and speak any language he chose through me. I had such power on me and in me as I never had before. And last but not least, I had a depth of love and sweetness in my soul that I had never even dreamed of before, and a holy calm possessed me, and a holy peace, that is deep and sweet beyond anything I ever experienced before, even in the sanctified life. And oh, such victory as he gives me all the time....

Now they just exclaim, "Brother Durham has got his Pentecost." Glory to God.

❧

Charles Finney

"I literally bellowed out the unutterable gushings of my heart."

Known as the "Father of Modern Revivalism" and "the first professional evangelist," Charles Grandison Finney (1792–1875) was born in Warren, Connecticut. As a young man Finney had a desire to practice law, and at age twenty attended Warren Academy in preparation for further legal studies at Yale College. In 1818 he moved to New York and began working for a judge as well as arguing several cases in the local justice courts.

After his dramatic conversion to Christ in 1821, he claimed that he had been given a "retainer from the Lord Jesus Christ *to plead his cause.*" He immediately switched gears by taking up the study of theology and was licensed to preach in 1823; a year later he was ordained in the Presbyterian Church. Later as a Congregationalist, he pastored the Broadway Tabernacle in New York City and brought fiery evangelistic preaching to many towns in the Northeast.

After coming to Oberlin College in 1835, Finney and college President Asa Mahan developed the "Oberlin Theology," which presaged the later "Higher Life" and pentecostal movements.

Finney's 1821 conversion testimony included what he called "a mighty baptism of the Holy Ghost." Pentecostals have often pointed to the phrase "I literally bellowed out the unutterable gushings of my heart" as a possible instance of speaking in tongues. Here in his own words is Finney's testimony.

There was no fire, and no light, in the room; nevertheless it appeared to me as if it were perfectly light. As I went in and shut the door after me, it seemed as if I met the Lord Jesus Christ face to face. It did not occur to me then, nor did it for some time afterward, that it was wholly a mental state. On the contrary it seemed to me that I saw him as I would see any other man.

He said nothing, but looked at me in such a manner as to break me right down at his feet. I have always since regarded this as a most remarkable state of mind; for it seemed to me a reality, that he stood before me, and I fell down at his feet and poured out my soul to him. I wept aloud like a child, and made such confessions as I could with my choked utterance. It seemed to me that I bathed his feet with my tears; and yet I had no distinct impression that I touched him, that I recollect.

I must have continued in this state for a good while; but my mind was too much absorbed with the interview to recollect anything that I said. But I know, as soon as my mind became calm enough to break off from the interview, I returned to the front office, and found that the fire that I had made of large wood was nearly burned out. But as I turned and was about to take a seat by the fire, I received a mighty baptism of the Holy Ghost.

Without any expectation of it, without ever having the thought in my mind that there was any such thing for me, without any recollection that I had ever heard the thing mentioned by any person in the world, the Holy Spirit descended upon me in a manner that seemed to go through me, body and soul. I could feel the impression, like a wave of electricity, going through and through me. Indeed it seemed to come in waves and waves of liquid love, for I could not express it in any other way. It seemed like the very breath of God. I can recollect distinctly that it seemed to fan me, like immense wings.

No words can express the wonderful love that was shed abroad in my heart. I wept aloud with joy and love; and I do not know but I should say, I literally bellowed out the unutterable gushings of my heart. These waves came over me, and over me, and over me, one after the other, until I recollect I cried out, "I shall die if these waves continue to pass over me." I said, "Lord, I cannot bear any more"; yet I had no fear of death.

How long I continued in this state, with this baptism continuing to roll over me and go through me, I do not know.

After his "baptism of the Holy Spirit," Finney saw extraordinary results in his preaching. In a revival in the town of Sodom, New York, he described the scene when "Power from on High" fell in the meeting.

The power from on high came down upon them in such a torrent that they fell from their seats in every direction. In less than a minute nearly the whole congregation were either down on their knees, or on their faces, or in some position before God. Everyone was crying or groaning for mercy upon his own soul. They paid no further attention to me or to my preaching. I tried to get their attention but I could not ...

❧

Alice Reynolds Flower

"Heavenly music poured forth like strains through the pipes of some great organ."

Singing in the Spirit has accompanied every stage of the pentecostal revival from Azusa Street days to the present-day charismatic renewal movement. Alice Reynolds Flower (1890–1991) was the wife of Joseph Flower, the founding secretary of the Assemblies of God. Throughout her long life, Alice experienced many manifestations of speaking in tongues that were recognized as known languages. She was honored as a leading figure in the Assemblies of God for decades before her death in 1991.

The following testimony is a first-person account of Alice Flower singing in tongues in a meeting led by "Brother Tom" Hezmalhalch, a Wesleyan Methodist minister. This happened in Los Angeles at the time Alice was baptized in the Holy Spirit on April 21, 1907.

We were taught to court the Spirit's moving and through the intervening years the urgency of this has greatly dominated my personal life along various lines of ministry. There were no ruts to our training, no spiritual habits; we were encouraged to expect a fresh working of God in any service, noting whichever direction the heavenly winds blew and learning to trim our sails accordingly.

Just a week after receiving the Comforter I had my first experience of singing in the heavenly choir. A brother was testifying at some length when Brother Tom interrupted him: "Hold on, brother; God is seeking to move in our midst." The brother stopped, then continued. Again Brother Tom checked him, kindly but firmly. Then we heard it—a low humming that gradually rose in harmonious crescendo as six individuals in different parts of the audience rose spontaneously to their feet and a full tide of glorious melody poured forth in ecstatic worship and praise.

Having been one of that group I can still feel the thrill as, for the first time, from my innermost being heavenly music poured forth like strains through the pipes of some great organ. No effort, no self-consciousness—just the flowing forth of celestial harmony like a fore-taste of divine rapture. Thanks be to God for the many times this holy joy has been repeated. Brother Tom had sensed God's desire and simply made room for his working.

Often I have thanked God for the example, the precepts of Brother Tom in my early years of pentecostal living and practice. He has been in glory these many years, but his godly influence lives on in my life and others who knew him.

When God takes over, what marvelous refreshing and divine accomplishment comes to his people in mere moments of time. No wonder we cry out in these days of increasing formality and oftentimes too-rigid organization, "Oh that thou wouldest rend the heavens, that thou wouldest come down, that the mountains might flow down at thy presence" (Is 64:1-2).

Many years later, at the Pentecostal Fellowship of North America annual convention in October 1964 in Springfield, Missouri, Alice Flower gave a manifestation of tongues in the Women's Auxiliary luncheon. Here is an account of that occasion.

Mrs. Alice Reynolds Flower gave an utterance in another language.

As she began, Mrs. J.W. Kofsman came to attention. With her husband, Mrs. Kofsman has lived and ministered in Jerusalem, Israel, for many years and knows the Hebrew language well. She heard Mrs. Flower speaking in the modern Hebrew language!

"I am the Messiah," Mrs. Flower was saying in a language she had never studied and did not know. Continuing in Hebrew, she exhorted the women to be out laboring for Christ while they had the opportunity, since the night was coming when the opportunity would no longer be theirs.

When Mrs. Flower began to speak in English, Mrs. Kofsman, the only one there who understood Hebrew, wondered if the interpretation would be correct. At first, she was disappointed, for Mrs. Flower's message in English was not the same as it had been in Hebrew.

Then an abrupt change came in the tonal quality of the speaker's voice, and Mrs. Flower began to speak as though she was praying. From that point, Mrs. Kofsman said, the speaker gave an accurate interpretation in English of what she had said in Hebrew.

❧

St. Francis of Assisi

"New songs were sung, and the servants of God jubilated in melody of the Spirit."

There is perhaps no better example of a Spirit-filled saint in the Middle Ages than St. Francis of Assisi (1181–1226). He was a man who exemplified our Lord's instructions: "For whosoever shall give you a cup of water to drink in my name, because you belong to Christ, truly I say unto you, he shall not lose his reward" (see Mk 9:41). Caring for the ill, the poor, and the lepers, Francis was much like our twentieth-century Mother Teresa.

Not only did he have a sacrificial love for mankind, but he also longed to tell everyone of the sacrifice of Christ and of God's offer of salvation to all. His standing motto was "Preach at all times, and if necessary, use words." And preach he did. St. Francis would always speak of the love of God ... while eating, while walking down the streets, while on the street corners.

He would even preach to animals he encountered. It was said that he would sometimes command whole flocks of birds to fly down and settle near him while he would tell them to clap their wings in praise for their wonderful Creator, almighty God. The birds would obey, and at his command take their leave of him.

Miraculous healings were very common at the touch of St. Francis' hand, and people would flock to him when he was in town. Although there are no records of his speaking in tongues, he is counted as one of the most striking charismatics in the history of the church.

In 1228, two years after the death of St. Francis in 1226, Pope Gregory IX arrived in Francis' birth city of Assisi to name him among the saints. The following account is by Francis' contemporary, Thomas Celano, who was no doubt an eyewitness. It shows the intense emotion of the occasion, which included jubilations (singing in the Spirit with "wordless" melodies of praise), shouting, and tears.

An account was read of the miracles and life of Francis. The Pope was so moved by this account that he "breathed deep sighs that rose from the bottom of his heart, and, seeking relief in repeated sobs, he shed a torrent of tears. The other prelates of the Church likewise poured forth a flood of tears, so that their sacred vestments were dampened by the abundant flow. Then all the people began to weep."

The Pope lifted up his hands to heaven and proclaimed Francis enrolled among the saints. "At these words the reverend cardinals, together with the Lord Pope, began to sing the Te Deum in a loud voice. Then there was raised a clamor among the many people praising God: the earth resounded with their mighty voices, the air was filled with their jubilations, and the ground was moistened with their tears.

"New songs were sung, and the servants of God jubilated in the melody of the Spirit. Sweet-sounding organs were heard there and spiritual hymns were sung with well-modulated voices. There a very sweet odor was breathed, and a most joyous melody that stirred the emotions resounded there."

<hr />

Billy Graham

"Here's what I want you to consider. Point number one I preached, point number two was the interpretation of the message in tongues verbatim and point number three was the benediction verbatim."

On December 9, 1982, Billy Graham (1918–) spoke at Evangel College in Springfield, Missouri, to some 3,000 students. This was a combined convocation with the students of the Assemblies of God Graduate School, Central Bible College, and Evangel College. Graham had come to Springfield, the headquarters city of the Assemblies of God, at the invitation of General Superintendent Dr. Thomas Zimmerman.

Because of time constraints caused by a scheduled press conference after the chapel service, Graham was forced to give only the first point of his message in the thirty minutes allotted. Before he could sit down, a student gave a clear message in tongues followed by an interpretation given by Pastor D.W. Wartenbee, Pastor of Bethel Assembly in Springfield. The benediction given by Evangel President Robert Spence closed the service. As it turned out, the tongues and interpretation and the benediction completed the second and third points of Graham's planned message.

Later, on nationwide television, Graham spoke of this event as one of the "three greatest miracles" he had witnessed in his entire ministry.

The following is the eyewitness account of the event as told by Sam Kaunley, a state trooper assigned by the State of Missouri to guard Graham during his trip to Springfield.

Here's the story. In 1982 Governor Christopher Bonds assigned executive security to Dr. Billy Graham while he was in Springfield, Missouri, speaking at a series of meetings. My name is Sam Kaunley, a state trooper for the state of Missouri at that time.

Dr. Graham arrived in Springfield at the Springfield regional airport and I picked him up there. He was traveling with Dr. Wilson. I picked up Dr. Wilson and Dr. Graham and stayed with them while they were in Springfield.

He was speaking at different places at the Assemblies of God headquarters, at a banquet, and at some other functions. But the main speaking engagement was to be held in the afternoon at Evangel University (then known as Evangel College).

Evangel University's chapel holds about 3,000 people, I believe, and of course every seat was filled. Dr. Graham was told that the schedule would include a special song and an introduction to Dr. Graham and that he would be preaching. The only stipulation was that because of a press conference and time for the media to get it on the air, the preaching would be held to thirty minutes so that they could move to the back of the chapel to the press conference and then from there to other functions.

Dr. Graham preached that day under a powerful anointing. After he preached the message, right at the very end of his message, before he stepped back from the podium, as I was standing on the platform by him, to the left in the back of the Evangel College chapel up in the back area, there was a man who stood and gave a message in tongues. Immediately following that message in tongues, over on the right top balcony area another man stood and gave an interpretation of the message in tongues that had been given.

It was not a long message in tongues and not a long interpretation. Without anything else said, one of the preachers, I think it was Dr. Robert Spence, who was the President of Evangel University, walked up to the podium and gave the benediction, and it was a short sentence.

We proceeded from there to the back of the auditorium, where the press was waiting and there was a fifteen- or twenty-minute press conference. After the press conference, Dr. Thomas Zimmerman, who was the General Superintendent of the Assemblies of God, and Dr. Wilson, the driver, and myself got into the car to go to the next location. There was the driver in the front seat with Dr. Wilson. In the back seat was Dr. Zimmerman, in the middle was Dr. Graham, and on the rear passenger side, myself.

As soon as the driver began to back out of the parking place, Dr. Graham was the first one to speak, and it was obvious that he was moved. He then said to his friend, "T.W., I want you to consider something."

Dr. Wilson turned sideways in his seat and looked back at him and said, "What's that?"

"You know, T.W., for years we have debated and discussed the baptism in the Holy Spirit with the evidence of speaking in tongues."

Dr. Wilson said, "Yes."

"T.W., I want you to consider this today. I had thirty minutes to preach this message and I had three points and I was going to preach those three points in thirty minutes; but I was moved on by the power and by the anointing of God to preach, and I only got point number one.

"Only point number one was preached. And, when I concluded my message, because of the time constraint of thirty minutes to go to the press conference, there was a man who stood up and gave a message in tongues, and did you hear that?"

"Yes, I did."

"There was a man over on the other side who stood up and gave the interpretation—he interpreted this message in tongues; did you hear that?"

"Yes, I did."

"After that, Dr. Spence came to the platform and gave the benediction."

"Yes, sir."

Billy Graham then looked at Dr. Wilson and said, "Here's what I want you to consider: Point number one I preached; point number two was the interpretation of the message in tongues verbatim; and point number three was the benediction verbatim."

Pastor Wartenbee's Interpretation:

Well, then it happened, someone on the first floor—I found out later they said it was a student—gave a lengthy tongue. And standing by my friend I sensed a powerful anointing of the Spirit of God. My body actually shook—I could control it, but I just felt such a heavy anointing. And I began in faith telling of the Lord of the harvest's great love for the souls and the church in Russia, and in China, and in other communist countries. And I said, "Pray, pray, pray ye the Lord of the harvest that he would thrust forth some of you in this building into the harvest field."

After the Graham visit, the General Superintendent of the Assemblies of God, Thomas Zimmerman, gave a report to the Board of Missions.

Brother Zimmerman shared some of the many favorable comments he had received from those attending the reception and banquet held in honor of Billy Graham. He also commented on the impression made upon Dr. Graham during the convocation held at Evangel College regarding the message in tongues and interpretation. This was particularly significant in that the interpretation given finished the message that Dr. Graham was unable to complete. Brother Zimmerman stated that he felt that the Lord used the situation to give validity to the gifts of the Spirit in operation.

~

Elena Guerra

"Grant us a long-awaited renewal of the face of the earth."

Elena Guerra (1833–1914), founder of the Oblate Sisters of the Holy Spirit, was born in Lucca, Italy in 1833. Developing a devotion to the Holy Spirit after becoming a nun, she was pained because she heard and read so little about the Holy Spirit in the life of the Catholic Church. When she was fifty years old, she felt constrained to write the pope concerning her desire to bring more attention to the Holy Spirit in the preaching and teaching of the church.

Although she was discouraged from writing the pontiff, she finally sent her first letter to Pope Leo XIII in 1895, calling for renewed preaching on the Holy Spirit "who is the One who forms the saints." In the last part of the letter she asserted that "Satan's empire will be broken by the Spirit" and that God would "grant us a long-awaited renewal of the face of the earth." This was the first of twelve confidential letters she sent to the pope between 1895 and 1903.

In these letters, Guerra called for a universal annual *novena* (nine-day cycle of prayers and meditations) to the Holy Spirit between the feasts of Ascension and Pentecost. This was to remember the ten days in the Cenacle (Upper Room) where the apostles tarried for the Holy Spirit, which was poured out on the day of Pentecost with fire, wind, and speaking in tongues. To promote the movement she founded "Permanent Cenacles," which were organized across Italy. In a subsequent letter to the Pope she explained her passion.

It is said that your Holiness places great hopes in a religious effort of prayer to the divine Paraclete (Holy Spirit). I take on myself to insist that this union of prayer to the Holy Spirit is exactly that which I dare to ask, but even more, that it be a permanent union, organized and proclaimed for the whole Church.

To this she added:

Oh, if ever the "Come, Holy Spirit," which, since the Cenacle and after, the Church has not ceased repeating, could become as popular as the "Hail Mary."

In another letter, Guerra stated:

Pentecost is not over. In fact it is continually going on in every time and every place, because the Holy Spirit desired to give himself to all men, and all who want him can always receive him, so we do not have to envy the apostles and the first believers; we only have to dispose ourselves like them to receive him well, and he will come to us as he did to them.

In 1897, Pope Leo XIII issued the most elaborate and detailed document on the Holy Spirit ever produced by a pope, entitled *Divinum Illud Munus,* in which he recommended a special devotion to the Holy Spirit by all Christians as well as directing that the annual novena be observed in all parishes. This would, he said, "bring about Christian unity among churches and the conversion of the universe."

In October 1900 Guerra wrote the Pope again and suggested that he open the new century by singing the ancient hymn *Veni Creator Spiritus* ("Come, Holy Spirit"). On January 1, 1901, the Pope sang the hymn in Rome to open the new century in honor of the Holy Spirit. On the same day that Pope Leo XIII sang this hymn, Agnes Ozman was baptized in the Holy Spirit in Topeka, Kansas, and spoke in tongues. This was the "touch felt round the world" that ushered in the twentieth century pentecostal movement.

Guerra's influence did not end at her death in 1914. When John XXIII became pope, the first saint to be beatified under his reign was Elena Guerra. When he called for the Second Vatican II in 1965, he asked every Catholic in the world to pray a daily prayer for the council, which began with words that would have gladdened the heart of Elena Guerra: "Renew your wonders in this our day as by a new Pentecost."

Two years after the end of Vatican II, the Catholic charismatic renewal began in Duquesne University in Pittsburgh, Pennsylvania, thus fulfilling the prophetic burdens of both Elena Guerra and Pope John XXIII.

The following is the text of Guerra's meditation and prayer for the first day of the novena to the Holy Spirit:

The Holy Spirit Acts in Us

The action of the Holy Spirit in souls makes us stand in wonder and awe, the more we come to know and contemplate it. Inaccessible by nature, out of his infinite goodness the Holy Spirit becomes accessible to hearts that are open and well-disposed, and communicates with them in an arcane and inexplicable way. He fills them and lets them feel his presence with light, inspiration, comforting and supernatural joy.

Prayer: O Holy Spirit, eternal Love, may the light of which you are origin and source open the eyes of my mind and allow me to know the effects of the infinite love you bear me better so as to move my heart to a sincere and faithful correspondence.

Lord, send forth your Spirit to renew the face of the earth.

❧

Madame Jeanne Guyon

"Thy love, O my God! Flowed in me like delicious oil, and burned as a fire which was going to destroy all that was left of self in an instant."

Madame Jeanne Guyon (1648–1717) was born in the village of Montargis, France. At the tender age of fifteen she was forced to marry an invalid man who was thirty-eight years old. With an unhappy marriage, she retreated into a devotional life that brought her true happiness. Because of her writings, she incurred the opposition of her religious superiors and was confined to a convent under royal order for one year. She was criticized for being a "quietist," or one who waits passively to hear from God. She then was imprisoned in the infamous Bastille for almost twenty-five years.

During these years, she wrote many devotional books that have become classics to Christians the world over. Above all, Madame Guyon wanted her readers to experience the living presence of Jesus Christ through prayer and the reading of the Scriptures. Over the years since her death, Guyon's work has been read and recommended by many great spiritual leaders including John Wesley, Francois Fenelon, Hudson Taylor, and others.

Through Wesley, Guyon enjoyed great influence in the Holiness movement of the late nineteenth century. Although she was a Catholic, she was included in James Gilchrist Lawson's famous book *Deeper Experiences of Famous Christians,* a veritable textbook for pre-pentecostals in the radical Wesleyan tradition. Her emphasis on "praying the Scripture" presaged the faith message of Kenneth Hagin and Kenneth Copeland.

In 1668, a Franciscan brother convinced her that "true religion was a matter of the heart and soul rather than a mere routine of ceremonial duties as she had supposed." Then she described her vivid spiritual experience:

Having said these words, the Franciscan left me. They were to me like the stroke of a dart, which pierced my heart asunder. I felt at this instant deeply wounded with the love of God—a wound so delightful that I desired it might never be healed. These words brought into my heart what I had been seeking so many years; or rather they made me discover what was there, and which I did not enjoy for want of knowing it.

Later she says:

I told this that my heart was quite changed; that God was there; for from that moment He had given me an experience of His presence in my soul—not merely as an object intellectually perceived by the application of the mind, but as a thing really possessed after the sweetest manner. I experienced those words in the Canticles: "Thy name is as a precious ointment poured forth; therefore do the virgins love thee." For I felt in my soul an unction, which, as a salutary perfume healed in a moment all my wounds. I slept not all that night, because Thy love, O my God! flowed in me like delicious oil, and burned as a fire which was going to destroy all that was left of self in an instant. I was all on a sudden so altered, that I was hardly to be known either to myself or others.

Madam Guyon was twenty years of age when she received this definite assurance of salvation through faith in Christ. It was on July 22, 1668. After this experience, she says:

Nothing was more easy to me now than to practice prayer. Hours passed away like moments, while I could hardly do anything else but pray. The fervency of my love allowed me no intermission. It was a prayer of rejoicing and of possession, wherein the taste of God was so great, so pure, so unblended and uninterrupted, that it drew and absorbed the powers of the soul into a profound recollection, a state of confiding and affectionate rest in God, existing without intellectual effort.

Some time later she said to the Franciscan:

I love God far more than the most affectionate lover among men loves the object of his earthly attachment. This love of God occupied my heart so constantly and strongly, that it was very difficult for me to think of anything else. Nothing else seemed worth attention.... I bade farewell forever to assemblies which I had visited, plays and diversions, to dancing, to unprofitable walks, and to parties of pleasure. The amusements and pleasures which are so much prized and esteemed by the world now appeared to me dull and insipid—so much so, that I wondered how I ever could have enjoyed them.

Kenneth Hagin

"Be thou faithful, for the time is short."

Kenneth E. Hagin (1917–) was born in Texas, prematurely and with a deformed heart. He was not expected to live. After fifteen years as an invalid, he was converted on April 22, 1933.

Hagin then began a pastoral ministry in a small independent church attended by Southern Baptists. In 1937 he was baptized in the Holy Spirit and entered the ranks of the pentecostals. In 1949 he began an itinerant ministry as a teacher and evangelist.

Hagin's ministry was radically changed in 1950 when he experienced a vision of Jesus, who gave him a commission to begin a healing ministry. From this time to 1963, he experienced eight visions, each of which expanded his ministry. He soon saw his healing ministry explode around the nation through tent meetings and radio ministries. By the early 1970s he became a favorite speaker for charismatics in many churches, including Roman Catholics.

During this time Hagin also became a leader in the "Word of Faith" or "positive confession" movement, where he influenced many young pastors and evangelists such as Kenneth Copeland. In 1974, he established the Rhema Bible Training Center in Tulsa, Oklahoma, where thousands of students came to study his faith message.

Hagan recalls a vision of Jesus on September 2, 1950, while he was preaching in a tent revival in Rockwall, Texas.

"Stand up on your feet," he [Jesus] said. As I stood before him again, he told me that I had entered into the second phase of my ministry in January 1950, and at that time he had spoken to me by prophecy and by the still small voice in my heart. He then talked to me about the other phases of my ministry.

Then the Lord said to me, "Stretch forth thine hand!" He held his own hands out before him. I did as he instructed and held my hands out in front of me. He placed the finger of his right hand in the palm

73

of my right hand, and then my left. The moment he did, my hands began to burn as if a coal of fire had been placed in them.

Then Jesus told me to kneel down before him. When I did so, he laid his hand upon my head, saying that he had called me and given me a special anointing to minister to the sick. He went on to instruct me that when I would pray and lay hands on the sick, I was to lay one hand on each side of the body.

If I felt the fire jump from hand to hand, an evil spirit or demon was present in the body causing the affliction. I should call it out in Jesus' name, and the demon or demons would have to go. If the fire, or anointing, in my hands did not jump from hand to hand, it was a case of healing only. I should pray for the person in his name, and if the person would believe and accept it, the anointing would leave my hands and go into that person's body, driving out the disease and bringing healing. When the fire, or the anointing, left my hands and went into the person's body, I would know he was healed....

Jesus then said, "Go thy way, son. Fulfill thy ministry and be thou faithful, for the time is short."

Jack Hayford

"Speak to him in tongues."

In his youth, Jack Williams Hayford, Jr. (1934–) and his family attended several evangelical churches, including the International Church of the Foursquare Gospel and the Christian and Missionary Alliance. Casting his lot with the pentecostals, Hayford attended L.I.F.E. Bible College in Los Angeles. After a pastorate in Indiana, he served as national Youth Director for the Foursquare Church and president of L.I.F.E. Bible College before settling down in 1969 as pastor of the First Foursquare Church in Van Nuys, California. As pastor, he made the church famous as "The Church on the Way," named for the Sherman Way Boulevard where the church is located.

Since that time he has become one of the best known and most respected pastors in America. His influence goes far beyond the borders of the pentecostal movement and reaches deep into the heart of the evangelical and mainline churches. A talented writer and gifted communicator, Hayford has become a major voice for pentecostals and charismatics around the world. In addition, he has written hundreds of hymns and worship songs, including the well-known chorus "Worship His Majesty." He also is founder of The King's Seminary in Van Nuys.

The following is his account of speaking to an airplane passenger in a language he (Hayford) did not know:

It is unquestionably one of the most disarming and remarkable experiences of my life as a Christian!

I had hardly seated myself in the first-class cabin when a well-dressed man in a business suit slid his briefcase into the overhead compartment and took his seat beside me. Even though I had anticipated privacy and a time for prayerful meditation while flying above such natural splendor as lay ahead, I greeted the man (let's call him Bill) and a casual conversation began.

"I was raised in Oklahoma, and my mother was a full-blooded Indian of the Kiowa tribe. When I started to school, I was still limited

in my English, and I think I still feel a kind of hangover embarrassment going back to when the kids used to mock me in school."

That's when it happened.

The instant he spoke those words, another set of words whispered within my heart, Speak to him in tongues. *It happened so quickly, and the prompting was so startling in its implications, I simply let the thought register in my mind but took no immediate action.*

"Bill," I said, "I've been sitting here with the most curious thought. I wonder ..." I hesitated. "I wonder—you know, quite a long time ago I was 'taught' some words in a language I don't know. And thinking about your familiarity with your native Kiowa Indian tongue, just out of curiosity—as I said, I wondered if you would mind if I said some of those words, just on the chance that you might recognize their meaning."

"Sure," he responded, without the least hesitation. "Go ahead." I looked away from his face, my eyes focused on the upholstery pattern on the back of the seat in front of him, and in a conversational tone began to speak in my spiritual language. I had hardly begun when it seemed I turned a linguistic corner, and I heard myself speaking a language unlike any I'd heard in prayer before. The total length of all I spoke was approximately the length of this paragraph. I stopped and looked back at Bill.

His response was immediate and businesslike. "That's a pre-Kiowan language, from which our Kiowa Indian tongue came." I remained amazingly composed, even though everything inside me wanted to shout, "IT IS?!—HALLELUJAH!" He continued: "I don't know all the words you spoke, but I do know the idea they express...." I could hardly believe what he was saying—I was overwhelmed, yet totally reserved in my outward demeanor.

"What are they about?" I asked.

"Well," he gestured in an upward fashion with his hand. "It's something about the light that's coming down from above."

It was a Holy Spirit setup ...

❧

G.T. Haywood

"The burning, convicting power of a pentecostal testimony filled the room."

Garfield Thomas Haywood (1880–1932), an African-American pastor from Indianapolis, was the single most important Oneness Pentecostal leader after the "New Issue" over the Godhead split the Assemblies of God in 1916. The Oneness or "Jesus Name" Pentecostal movement was pioneered by Glenn Cook and Frank Ewart in California in 1913 and soon spread throughout the United States. In 1916, after being rejected by the Assemblies of God, Haywood and his large church in Indianapolis became the center of the movement through the organization of the Pentecostal Assemblies of the World (PAW). The first leader of the new church was Elder G.T. Haywood, who led the church until his death in 1932.

Although the PAW was completely interracial in its beginnings, with about equal numbers of white and black pastors, the movement ultimately split on racial lines in 1924, with the white pastors ultimately organizing the United Pentecostal

Church in 1945. During his remarkable ministry, Haywood built a large congregation, Christ Church, in Indianapolis, and wrote hundreds of hymns and gospel songs, all while serving as the leader of a major denomination.

The following is an account of his baptism in the Holy Spirit in 1908 prior to his coming into contact with the Oneness teaching.

In the cold bleak month of February 1908, there dropped into the life of G.T. Haywood a never-to-be-forgotten witness for the Lord. This man, Otis Barber, had a personal testimony that burned within his soul. He had just visited a pentecostal service and had been filled with the Holy Ghost with the evidence of speaking in tongues.

Barber visited Haywood in his home and began to tell him of his new experience. Outside the house a cold damp Indiana winter gripped the countryside, but inside the house the burning, convicting power of a pentecostal testimony filled the room. The pentecostal fire that burned in Barber's heart as he spoke of the apostolic experience opened the spiritually cold heart of Haywood, and conviction gripped his soul. He heard Barber's message with an open heart and fully made up his mind that he, too, was going to receive the baptism of the Holy Ghost.

His mind made up, Haywood made plans to attend the pentecostal services that his friend Barber attended. The main worry of Haywood was whether his wife would follow him in seeking the baptism of the Holy Ghost. This worry was not relieved when she and her sister decided to attend the services with him, for they were not going with the thought of seeking the Lord, but rather to watch and see what would happen to Haywood as he sought the Holy Ghost.

During the service that night Haywood, his wife, and sister sat at the very back of the church. As the sermon concluded, Otis Barber made his way to the back of the church and asked Haywood the simple question, "Won't you come and get the Holy Ghost tonight, Tom?"

With that request, Haywood stepped out and made an unforgettable trip down to that old-fashioned altar. The power of God soon fell, and Gladstone Thomas Haywood entered into a new life in Jesus Christ. The heavy burden and guilt of sin was washed away as all things became new. The blood of Calvary's lamb had done its cleansing work....

There was more in store for that night, and while Haywood was under the power of God at the altar, Otis Barber returned to the back of the church and invited Haywood's wife and sister to the altar. They did not get up and start towards the altar as Haywood had done, but the convicting power of the Holy Ghost began to move. Suddenly, the power of God fell upon both of them where they were sitting. They fell to the floor and in a few minutes began to speak in other tongues as the Spirit of God took control of their lives. What a glorious day as the angels of heaven recorded three names in the Book of Life.

∽

Nickles J. Holmes

"In a short time the Spirit was manifested in marvelous ways.... Pentecost had indeed come to Altamont."

Nickles John Holmes (1847–1919), who was born in Spartanburg, South Carolina, studied law at Edinburgh University in Scotland from 1865 to 1868 with the desire of becoming a lawyer. After returning to the United States, however, he felt called to enter the Presbyterian ministry. After his ordination in 1888, he served as pastor of the Second Presbyterian Church in Greenville, South Carolina.

At this time he became interested in the "higher life" movement and journeyed to Northfield, Massachussetts, to learn more from Dwight L. Moody. In July 1896, he received a sanctification experience and entered wholeheartedly into the ranks of the Holiness movement.

By 1898 he had organized the Tabernacle Presbyterian Church in Greenville, which became a center for holiness revival. He also began teaching Bible classes on Parris Mountain outside of Greenville, which became the beginnings of Holmes Bible College. At that time the school was called "Altamont Bible Institute."

In 1907, Holmes went to hear G.B. Cashwell preach in Union, South Carolina. Cashwell had just returned from Azusa Street, where he spoke in tongues under the ministry of William J. Seymour. He was now a fiery pentecostal evangelist. Holmes returned to his school hungry for his own personal pentecostal experience.

The following testimony is his account of how he and many of the students experienced not only tongues, but singing, dancing, playing the organ, and writing in the Spirit.

Then as my heart was going up for the Holy Ghost, it seemed that the whole room was filled with a mist of heaven, and my whole body was being permeated by it. And a great roll of mist above my head as a waterfall, only it was still not falling. As I prayed for the gifts of the Spirit, they seemed to stand out before me in bold relief just as if they were waiting to be received, and when I came to the word faith, it seemed to stand out in large capital letters, and I felt that I almost had them and would have them, but not at that moment. I thought, surely this is indeed Pentecost.

I recognized the presence and power of the Holy Ghost in all this, and as soon as I recovered the control of my mouth I testified and praised God for Pentecost—the baptism with the Holy Ghost. The Holy Ghost came to abide within me. He gave me at that time only the very rudiments of language, the motioning of my tongue and chattering of my teeth.

Afterwards I jabbered and then spoke words. I had the witness with my tongue to the baptism, but not the gift of tongues, neither do I claim the gift of tongues yet, though I speak in tongues. The gift of tongues (see 1 Cor 12), is of diverse kinds of tongues, according to the Greek, births of tongues, languages born in you. This is I believe a permanent gift, and may or may not be exercised at will, but whether at will or not it is all under the power of the Holy Ghost, for no man can speak a language unknown to him in his own power. It must be the supernatural power of God that enables him to speak, even though he speak at will.

The students went to the altar with an earnestness that they had not manifested before. The Holy Spirit began working immediately. They began to pray and praise God, and in a short time the Spirit was manifested in marvelous ways, some of them here and there in the tent began to rise up speaking in tongues. Some began to write in an unknown language, some were singing in other tongues, others dancing and others playing on the organ under the power of the Spirit. Pentecost had indeed come to Altamont.

Willis C. Hoover

"From over there they are calling me."

One of the most striking pentecostal revivals of the twentieth century took place in the Methodist Episcopal Church of Chile in 1909. The head of the Church in Chile at the time was the American missionary Willis Collins Hoover (1858–1936) who had arrived in Chile from Chicago in 1889, building on the foundations laid by the Methodist-Holiness missionary statesman William Taylor. Although Hoover was a certified medical doctor, he went to Chile with no theological training.

In 1909 Hoover was pastor of the Methodist Church in Valparaiso when several leaders began to pray for revival every day at the 5:00 P.M. tea time. At this time Hoover read reports of manifestations of tongues and healing in India through an old friend, Minnie F. Abrams. Soon amazing pentecostal manifestations began to occur in his church, including tongues, visions, dreams, healings, and words of knowledge. A leader in the revival was a young English woman, Nellie Laidlaw, who functioned as a prophetess in the revival.

In 1910, the Methodist Episcopal Church forced the resignation of Hoover, who with thirty-seven Chilean followers organized the Pentecostal Methodist Church of Chile. By the year 2000, the Pentecostals of Chile had grown to be the largest Protestant church in the nation, with some estimates of over 2,000,000 members.

The following testimony is from Maria Pino de Navarrete concerning some of the extraordinary events that took place in 1909. It describes the progress of the revival and the first instance of speaking in tongues, which occurred on July 4, 1909.

There were many proud young ladies that fell to the floor in a heap. Mrs. Hoover took charge of covering their legs with shawls and jackets. Mr. Hoover had the most spiritual people go to the side of the ones who had fallen to the floor to pray with them and to listen to what they were saying. Sometimes they had to call Mr. Hoover or some official of the church to be a witness, because that is what the people asked for. There were times when the brothers wanted there to be witnesses to what they said, who would then go with them afterwards to make retribution to the ones they had defrauded.

So, one of the first manifestations of the Holy Spirit was that they would fall to the ground. It was after this, when their vessel was all clean, that the Holy Spirit could then come upon them. Then they would start speaking in tongues.

The first person that spoke in tongues was a young lady. She was seated on a bench, leaning against Mrs. Hoover, who supported her. Rosa Pino, Natalia Arancibia, and other brothers and sisters and church faithful surrounded her wonderingly. This girl was speaking in tongues and nobody understood her. Then someone asked Mr. Hoover what language he thought she would be speaking in.

"It seems," said Mr. Hoover, "to be Greek or Hebrew."

When he said that, I, as a curious little girl, went squirming through the people until I could get to where she was, because she was my classmate. Then I had to climb up on a bench in order to see what everybody else was looking at, because everyone was looking toward the door of the church. There I saw a tall young lady entering the church on the arm of a gentleman. She was dressed very elegantly and was saying: "Who is calling me?"

Mr. Hoover went to receive them and said, "I don't know, Ma'am, who could be calling you."

"Yes, they called me, and they called me by my name."

Mr. Hoover later related that this lady explained to him that here in Chile she had another name. It wasn't her real name, but she had been called by her real name.

Then, when she heard that she was being called again, she said, "From over there they are calling me."

And it was that girl who was speaking in tongues who was calling her.

She was speaking in Greek.

The lady was a married lady who had left Greece with a Chilean sailor, and she had left her husband there. In Chile she was using another name.

She went over to where the girl was that was speaking in tongues and had called her. She told Mr. Hoover, weeping, that the girl had rebuked her for all the sins in her life from the time she was a young child. Furthermore, she told her to repent and get away from that man that was with her, and to return to the side of her husband. And if not, the hand of God would be upon her. She went back to Greece immediately, and from that time on, tongues started being manifest among the believers in Chile.

∾

Edward Irving

"This gift of tongues is the crowning act of all."

Edward Irving (1792–1834) was born in Annan, Scotland. He was educated at Edinburgh and in 1815 received a license to preach in the Scottish Presbyterian Church. Irving was a powerful orator, and his charismatic personality and zeal in preaching drew large crowds to his Regent Square Church. After studying the Scriptures intently Irving became convinced that God had never withdrawn the gifts of the Holy Spirit, and so he began preaching to this effect. In the meantime, Irving joined with other English evangelicals in studying prophecy since they believed that they were living in the very last days.

In time the group concluded that signs of the last days included the restoration of the gifts of the Spirit to the church as well as the fivefold ministries of apostle, prophet, pastor-teacher, and evangelist. All began looking for evidences that tongues were being restored to the church. In time, they found a small group near Glasgow, Scotland, who spoke in tongues and interpreted the messages into English. The leader of the group was Mary Campbell, whom Irving invited to attend his church in London.

On the morning of October 16, 1831, during a Sunday morning worship service, Mary Campbell burst loose and began speaking in an unknown tongue. This caused great confusion and placed a cloud of suspicion over Irving, who was later tried and dismissed from the Presbytery—not over the question of tongues, but over his Christology.

Later Irving joined with twelve other "apostles" in forming the "Catholic Apostolic Church." Although Irving was disappointed at not speaking in tongues himself, he saw tongues as the "standing sign of the Baptism in the Holy Ghost" and the "root and stem" out of which the other gifts flowed. Some have seen Irving as the most important precursor of the modern pentecostal movement, which began in 1901.

The following excerpts from Irving reflect some of his teachings on the gift of speaking in tongues.

We met together about two weeks before the meeting of the General Assembly, in order to pray that the General Assembly might be guided in judgement by the Lord, the head of the Church. We cried unto the Lord for apostles, prophets, evangelists, pastors, and teachers, anointed with the Holy Ghost the gift of Jesus, because we saw it written in God's word that these are the appointed ordinances for the edifying of the body of Jesus. We continued in prayer every morning, morning by morning, at half past six o'clock; and the Lord was not long in hearing and answering our prayer.

The unknown tongue, as it began its strange sounds, would be equal to a voice from the glory, "Thus said the Lord of Hosts," or "This is my Son, hear ye him"; and every ear would say, "Oh, that I knew the voice"; and when the man with the gift of interpretation gave it out in the vernacular tongue, we would be filled with an awe, that it was no other than God who had spoken it. Methinks it is altogether equal to the speaking with the trumpet from the thick darkness of the Mount, or with a voice as thunder from the open vault of heaven. The using of man's organs is indeed, a mark of a new dispensation, foretold as to come to pass after Christ ascended up on high, when he would receive gifts and bestow them on men, that the Lord God might dwell, might have an habitation, in them.

This gift of tongues is the crowning act of all. None of the old prophets had it, Christ had it not; it belongs to the dispensation of the Holy Ghost proceeding from the risen Christ: it is the proclamation that man is enthroned in heaven, that man is the dwelling-place of God, that all creation if they would know God, must give ear to man's tongue, and know the compass of reason. It is not we that speak, but Christ that speaketh. It is not in us as men that God speaks; but in us as members of Christ, as the Church and body of Christ, that God speaks. The honor is not to us, but to Christ; not to the Godhead of Christ, which is ever the same, but to the manhood of Christ, which hath been raised from the state of death to the state of being God's temple, God's most holy place, God's shechinah, God's oracle, for ever and ever.

I most solemnly warn you all, in the name of the Most High God, for no earthly consideration whatever, to gainsay or impede the work of speaking with tongues and prophesying, which God hath begun amongst us, and which answereth in all respects, both formally and spiritually, to the thing promised in the Scriptures to those who believe—possessed in the primitive church; and much prayed for by us all.

❧

Benjamin Hardin Irwin

"He caused me to use words which I had never heard or conceived of before."

Benjamin Hardin Irwin (1854–19??) was a pivotal figure in the transition of several radical Holiness movements to the pentecostal movement. In the early 1890s he led a "fire-baptized Holiness" movement in the Midwest, which culminated in the formation of a national body called the "Fire Baptized Holiness Association" in Anderson, South Carolina, in 1898.

The central teaching of the movement was that subsequent to the experiences of justification and entire sanctification a "third blessing" called "the fire" could be experienced by the earnest seeker. By 1900 the movement had spread across the United States and Canada. It was also distinguished by having black leadership in the highest levels of the organization. Later Irwin was known for teaching subsequent "baptisms" known as "Dynamite," "Oxidite," and "Lyddite."

Unfortunately, Irwin fell into moral failure in 1900 and resigned from the movement. Afterwards, remnants of his movement became integral parts of the Pentecostal Holiness Church and the Church of God headquartered in Cleveland, Tennessee.

By 1906, Irwin was in Salem, Oregon, with Azusa Street veteran Florence Crawford where on Christmas Eve, 1906, he not only renounced his earlier errors, but spoke in tongues, thereby becoming a practicing pentecostal.

His new theological understanding concerning the baptism in the Holy Spirit was typical of the Azusa Street era, which encompassed three "blessings."

My conception of the pentecostal baptism not only implied the experience of justification and entire sanctification as essential prerequisites, but the baptism itself includes the fullness of the Spirit AND the speaking with other tongues. The speaking in tongues is not simply the sign or evidence of the baptism, but a part of the divine baptism itself.

The following is Irwin's testimony of his pentecostal baptism in the Holy Spirit.

A supernatural tranquillity and unearthly sweetness, a divine assurance that the Holy Ghost, the promised Comforter, had come into my soul to abide forever, was then and there vouchsafed to me. I knew that I was filled with the Holy Spirit. Then it was that my soul "waited in silence for God only" (Ps 62:1).

I waited for God, the Holy Spirit, to speak through me. Then I felt my lips and tongue and lower jaw being used as they had never been used before. My vocal organs were in the hands and the control of another, and the Other was the Divine Paraclete within me. He was beginning to speak through me in other tongues.

I lay there and listened to the voice of the Holy Ghost. For nearly an hour he continued to speak in different unknown tongues. He caused me to use words which I had never heard or conceived of before. I was enabled to speak with greater fluency than I had ever spoken in my native English. I tried to remember or to retain some of the words, but could not, and to this day I cannot recall a single word.

I arose about midnight and went into the auditorium, where Mrs. Irwin, Sister Crawford, and one or two others still lingered, and testified to the baptism of the Holy Ghost and fire. But I did not speak in tongues to them. I could not do it of myself. I have never put forth the least effort to speak in unknown tongues. I can speak only "as the Spirit gives me utterance."

Since that time, I have been used of God in speaking many times in Chinese, Hindoostani, Bengali, Arabic, and other languages unknown to me.

∞

Stephen Jeffreys

"It is the Lord's doing, and like living in the Acts of the Apostles."

One of the greatest revivals of the twentieth century was the Welsh Revival of 1904–05. During that short time 100,000 souls were converted under the ministry started by evangelist Evan Roberts. So dramatic were the conversions of these mostly coal miners that pubs and gambling houses in the town of Loughor soon went out of business for lack of patrons.

Toward the end of his life Roberts was asked to name some people converted during the revival who went on to do great things for God. Without hesitation he replied, "Beyond all those I know—Stephen Jeffreys."

Stephen Jeffreys (1876–1943) was born in Nantyffyllon, South Wales, the third of twelve children. He was a coal miner who was converted during the great Welsh Revival. After his conversion he continued to work in the coal mines, witnessing to his fellow workers and conducting open-air preaching whenever and wherever he saw opportunity. God poured out a powerful anointing upon Jeffreys, and it was well known in Wales that if any were ill, all that they should do was bring the sick to the man of God—Stephen Jeffreys.

The healings that occurred in his ministry were truly miraculous and could not be denied. One Rev. J. W. Adams, the vicar of Wall, happened to be in town when a friend urged him to attend a meeting that Jeffreys was conducting. He attended and soon found out what all the inhabitants of Wales already knew—that God was among them. Rev. Adams later recalled that night.

In May 1925, Rev. J. W. Adams, the vicar of Wall, was in London for a week's vacation. He met a friend who urged him, "Go to the Surrey Tabernacle, Walworth, to see Stephen Jeffreys. Staid churchman as you are, you won't be there half an hour before you are shouting 'Hallelujah.'" Mr. Adams thought his friend seemed a little mentally off balance; nevertheless, he decided to go.

The visit persuaded him.

"I went as near to the front as space permitted and was soon profoundly impressed that he and his helpers were instruments of the Lord Jesus for healing cancer, tuberculosis, and all manner of sicknesses. After being given up by doctors and discharged from hospitals, certified incurable,... many before and after the laying on of hands [were] completely and some instantly healed. The blind received sight, the deaf heard, the dumb spoke, cancer was cured, and the lame ran and leaped for joy. Above all, the gospel was preached to poor and rich alike.

"I was within five feet of a little girl who had one good eye; but her left socket was empty and had in its rear a blank skin, something like

a thumbnail. I had just time to wonder what ailment her mother had brought her for, because she appeared to be in good physical health, when Pastor Jeffreys caught sight of my clerical collar and very kindly beckoned me on to the platform. Thus it was my good fortune when the child was brought up for the laying on of hands to be quite near her again.

"After a few seconds of earnest prayer, the pastor lifted his hands away and there was a beautiful new blue eye that resembled the other, and through which, after the other was blindfolded, she saw quite clearly. Whilst her sight was being tested, Mr. Jeffreys and the child's mother allowed me to touch and closely examine the girl.

"Friends have said, 'Did you really see the child before the new eye and afterwards?' Yes, I really did. It is amazing how doubters will cling to any shreds of excuse for unbelief.

"For instance, a hospital matron tried to brush it aside with, 'Probably there was an eye there all the time with a skin over that just needed slitting.' I replied, 'If that was all, why on earth did not one of the numerous doctors, to whom the child was taken, just slit it?' She gave no reply.

"At these healing services I was privileged to witness a hundred miracles in that one week. It is the Lord's doing, and like living in the Acts of the Apostles."

∾

Pope John Paul II

"This dimension of the faith has been diminished, indeed inhibited, scarcely there. Now we can say that this movement is everywhere, also in my country."

In one of his first audiences with Catholic charismatics, Pope John Paul II was shown a forty-minute tape of the enthusiastic worship experienced by charismatics. The meeting took place on December 11, 1979, in the Vatican, where the Pope met with leaders of the International Catholic Charismatic Renewal Organization (ICCRO).

His response to the talks, the gestures, the singing, and the praise was warm and immediate. Referring to the tape, he had this to say:

Thank you! It was an expression of faith. Indeed, the singing, the words, and the gestures. It is ... how does one say it? I can say that it is a revolution of this living expression [of the faith].

We say that the faith is a matter of the intelligence, and at times also of the heart, but this expressive dimension of the faith has been absent. This dimension of the faith has been diminished, indeed inhibited, scarcely there. Now we can say that this movement is everywhere, also in my country. But it is different there. In Poland, it is not so expressive as in the film, but it is still the same thing—something like another edition of the same book.

After this, there were introductions, greetings, and sharing of information about the renewal. Then the Pope made the following spontaneous comments:

This is my first meeting with you, Catholic charismatics. First, permit me to explain my own charismatic life.

I have always belonged to the renewal in the Holy Spirit. My own experience is very interesting. When I was in school, at the age of twelve or thirteen, sometimes I had difficulties in my studies, in particular with mathematics.

My father gave me a book on prayer. He opened it to a page and said to me: "Here you have the prayer to the Holy Spirit. You must say this prayer every day of your life."

I have remained obedient to this that my father gave nearly fifty years ago, which I believe is no little while. This was my first spiritual initiation, so I can understand all the different charisms. All of them are part of the riches of the Lord.

I am convinced that this movement is a sign of his action. The world is much in need of this action of the Holy Spirit; it needs many instruments for this action. The situation in the world is dangerous, very dangerous. Materialism is opposed to the true dimension of human power, and there are many different kinds of materialism. Materialism is the negation of the spiritual, and this is why we need the action of the Holy Spirit.

Now I see this movement, this activity everywhere. In my own country I have seen a special presence of the Holy Spirit. Through this action, the Holy Spirit comes to the human spirit, and from this moment we begin to live again, to find our very selves, to find our identity, our total humanity. Consequently, I am convinced that this movement is a very important component in the total renewal of the Church, in this spiritual renewal of the Church.

After the group joined in singing the *"Magnificat,"* the Pope left the room saying in Italian: *"Praised be Jesus Christ!"*

Joseph H. King

"Who has been sanctified? Raise your hand."

Joseph Hillary King (1869–1946) was the first bishop and long-time General Superintendent of the Pentecostal Holiness Church. His life ran the gamut of the Methodist, Holiness, and pentecostal movements of the late 1800s and early 1900s. Beginning as a Methodist in Georgia, he later joined and became leader of the Fire-Baptized Holiness Church. When the Fire-Baptized Holiness Church merged with the Pentecostal Holiness in 1911, he became the formative leader of that church from 1917 until his death in 1946.

In 1907, King was baptized in the Holy Spirit in Toccoa, Georgia, and spoke in tongues, thereby bringing his followers with him into the infant pentecostal movement. He is credited with coining the doctrinal phrase "initial evidence" in 1908 in reference to tongues as the sign of the baptism in the Holy Spirit. His major theological work was *From Passover to Pentecost* (1911), one of the earliest pentecostal doctrinal works. The following sanctification testimony was taken from his autobiography *Yet Speaketh*, which was published in 1949.

King's sanctification experience took place in the Carnesville Methodist Church in Northeast Georgia in 1885. He could recall the very day and hour. These Methodists and the Holiness people that followed them also called the sanctification experience a "baptism in the Holy Spirit," although speaking in tongues was not considered important until 1901 with the rise of the pentecostal movement. In this testimony, the word "consecration" refers to a surrender of a person's life to Christ; it was often a synonym for the sanctification experience.

I did not know what consecration was, nor how to make it. The great High Priest in heaven must have done it, since I was in a passive state before God. For the moment nothing took place in my heart. It did not occur to me to believe in the Lord for the cleansing of my heart. No, not one thought of faith entered my mind.

Mr. Hudson closed his reading and remarks upon consecration and sat down. Presently Mr. Gorham, the aged and venerable minister, arose and read a short collection from the book that he had written upon the same subject, and he said upon finishing the same paragraph, "That is consecration."

As he made the remark suddenly an indescribable scene occurred. The church was filled with the power and glory of God. Some began to rise and shout the high praises of God, while others laughed, cried, and gave glory to God.

A marvelous change was wrought in me. I found my heart filled with light, love, and glory. How it came into me I know not. I was no more conscious of exercising faith than I was of flying. I cannot explain it, but I know that I had the indescribable in me, and have never doubted it.

When the shouting ceased someone arose and asked, "Who has been sanctified? Raise your hand." My hand went up almost without an effort. Then I do not know what took place in the church, that is, I do not remember what the little audience did. I seemingly was taken out of myself and I thought I was within a few feet of the gates of heaven.

When I came to myself I was standing in the aisle in silence, but such glory that I felt was beyond what I had felt a few minutes before:

it was utterly indescribable. I was, as it were, in heaven. Peace unutterable filled my inner being. How could an angel feel any happier than I did in those moments!

This was Friday morning, October 23, 1885, a day, an hour, never to be forgotten by me. As I walked home about noon it seemed that earth was filled with heaven. All nature was singing the praises of the Lord. It seemed that I could see God as plainly as I saw visible things around me.

For months my life flowed on without disturbance. I was looking upon Jesus on the throne, which appeared to be not so far above me. I was as ready to live in heaven as upon earth. There was no fear of death or of meeting God. I cared for nothing but God, and wanted nothing but more of him. He was so real to me, and present with me. It can never be told.

After the pentecostal movement began to spread from Azusa Street after 1906, King and other Holiness leaders were forced to discern whether this was indeed a work of God. While serving as head of the Fire-Baptized Holiness Church, King also pastored the local congregation in Toccoa, Georgia. In January 1908 he invited G. B. Cashwell to preach in his church. At first King opposed the pentecostal teaching, but a study of the Greek New Testament convinced him to accept Cashwell's teaching. His low-key pentecostal experience of 1908 contrasted with his vivid sanctification experience of 1885.

The following is King's account of his baptism in the Holy Spirit on February 15, 1908.

As I was seeking, the scripture recorded in John 7:37-39 seemed to be applied to my heart, and I was persuaded to rest unreservedly upon this promise. There was a joy in my heart and I began uttering praise with my lips. There came into my heart something new though the manifestation was not great.

There was a moving of my tongue, though I cannot say that I was speaking a definite language. I only knew that there was some moving of my tongue as I had never experienced before. I had the assurance that the Comforter had come into my heart. There was a peace that permeated my spirit, and I was resting in the Lord in a very blessed manner. Soon the Word began to be opened to me in a new way, and it seemed as if I had a new Bible.

Kathryn Kuhlman

"He arose from his seat and walked without the support of his crutches. Instantly healed."

Kathryn Kuhlman (1907–76) was born on her parents' farm, five miles south of Concordia, Missouri, in 1907. She began preaching as a young teenager, and in her early meetings crowds would fill the pews and balconies to hear this simple, unschooled young woman talk about the grace of God. Years later word began to get out that people were being healed who attended her services. Before long thousands were flocking to her services. Men and women of all denominations and persuasions were lining up to be touched and prayed over by her.

Kathryn Kuhlman was a host of contradictions. She was fond of saying, "I believe in tongues. I believe every church in the nation should have tongues and interpretation." And yet Kathryn would never reveal whether she spoke in tongues, and her closest friends never reported hearing her pray in tongues, nor would she allow them in any of her miracle services. She spoke often against the sensationalism of pentecostal manifestations, and yet most of the people she prayed for were "slain in the Spirit" when she laid her hands on them—and that, much to her approval.

Of all the manifestations of the Spirit that occurred in her meetings the most notable, of course, were the healings. Regarding these she would simply say, "I have no healing virtue. I cannot heal a single person. All I do is preach faith. God does the healing. Whom he heals and whom he chooses not to heal is his business. I am but his handmaiden."

It has been estimated that she ministered to over 100,000,000 people in her fifty years of active ministry. Thousands upon thousands of people claimed healing in her "miracle services," and she was the most widely known female evangelist of her day. Yet she was also one of the most controversial figures within pentecostalism.

The following are Kuhlman's accounts of some of the miraculous claims made in her early ministry in Pittsburgh.

Miracles continued to happen. Paul R. Gunn, a young Pittsburgh policeman, had been taken to a local hospital on September 28, 1949, with viral pneumonia. A lung ailment was diagnosed as cancer following bronchoscope, sputum, and X-ray examinations.

In October he started attending the services at Carnegie Hall. During the fourth service he said he felt like a match had been struck to a piece of paper inside his chest. In December a company doctor approved him for work and he started back on his job in January, 1950.

James W. McCutcheon was another miracle. Three years before, he was standing on a timber which was struck by a bulldozer in Lorain, Ohio. He was thrown to the ground and the ball joint of his hip was crushed.

Five operations failed. The last one, a bone graft, was equally unsuccessful because of decalcification. The doctors recommended still another operation.

McCutcheon was on crutches when he entered Carnegie Hall on November 5, 1949. His daughter, sitting next to him with her hand on his knee, later said she felt something like electricity enter her arm from his leg while Miss Kuhlman was preaching. He arose from his seat and walked without the support of his crutches. Instantly healed.

It was four o'clock on a Saturday afternoon. It was at that time and in that place that I surrendered myself fully to the Holy Spirit.

There are some things too sacred to talk about. I will only say that in that moment, with tears streaming down my face, God and I made each other promises. He knows that I'll be true to him and I know that I'll be true to him. In that moment, I yielded to God in body, soul, and spirit. I gave him everything.

Then I knew what the scripture meant about taking up your cross. A cross is the symbol of death. That afternoon, Kathryn Kuhlman died. And when I died, God came in, the Holy Spirit came in. There, for the first time, I realized what it meant to have power.

Joan McCarthy

"Have you ever studied church languages?"

Since Roman Catholics have members from all over the world who speak many different languages, it was not unusual in the early days of the charismatic renewal for messages in tongues to be identified. The following testimony is an account of a prayer meeting in Ludington, Michigan, in June 1971 where a message in tongues was identified as Greek-Aramaic by scholars who were present.

The report was made to *New Covenant* magazine by Joan McCarthy, of Grand Haven, Michigan, and the Reverend Richard Lamphear of Ludington, Michigan.

A number of the people in the Grand Haven-Muskegon Roman Catholic prayer community traveled to Ludington for a prayer meeting with members of the St. Simon's Catholic Church. They hoped a similar prayer group in Ludington would result. About forty people were present, including Msgr. Arthur Bukowski, former president of Aquinas College, and Fr. Eugene Albesteffer, assistant priest at St. Simon's.

In the early part of the afternoon, Joan McCarthy, of Grand Haven, felt impressed to speak in other tongues. She was hesitant, however, because strangers were present. But finally she yielded to the influence of the Holy Spirit and did so.

Among those present at the meeting was Rev. Richard Lamphear, pastor of the Assemblies of God church in Ludington. He had become acquainted with the Roman Catholic friends of Ludington and had told them of his own experience of the baptism in the Holy Spirit. After Joan McCarthy finished her utterance, Pastor Lamphear—also inspired by the Holy Spirit—gave the interpretation. It was to the effect that the people from St. Simon's should be united in whichever course they chose to follow and should not divide themselves into groups. They would find their strength in unity, in their love to Christ and to one another.

As the meeting concluded, the leader, Bert Ghezzi, asked if there were any questions.

Fr. Albesteffer addressed Joan McCarthy: "Have you ever studied church languages?"

"No," she replied.

The priest asked Pastor Lamphear the same question and received the same reply.

Then Fr. Albesteffer said: "I know what speaking in tongues is from my study of Scripture, but this is the first time I have ever witnessed it. Joan, you spoke perfect, fluent Greek-Aramaic, the language believed to have been spoken by Christ Jesus. And, Reverend Lamphear, you gave an almost word-for-word translation of what she said."

∾

Francis MacNutt

"Sure enough, I fell—all six feet four inches of me."

Francis Scott MacNutt (1925–) was born in St. Louis, Missouri. After studying at Harvard for his B.A. degree, MacNutt received the M.F.A. at Catholic University and the Ph.D. at Aquinas Institute of Theology. For some years he served as a professor of homiletics and as president of the Catholic Homiletic Society. He was ordained into the Catholic priesthood in 1956.

Eleven years later, in 1967, he received the baptism in the Holy Spirit in an ecumenical retreat in Tennessee. He then focused on promoting the healing ministry of the Spirit to both his Catholic and Protestant brothers. By the late 1970s he was a popular speaker at charismatic conferences around the world. He was especially instrumental in helping to spread the charismatic renewal to other priests around the world. His ministry was notable for the many persons who were "slain in the Spirit" as a result of his prayers. In this he was greatly influenced by Kathryn Kuhlman.

The following is MacNutt's testimony of attending a Kuhlman meeting.

The first time I saw someone slain in the Spirit was in 1970.

I had heard a great deal about this curious phenomenon, about how people were touched by ministers who had this gift and just toppled over "under the power." I had talked to one priest who had been to a Kathryn Kuhlman meeting in Pittsburgh and was so sensitive to this power that he couldn't even get near her but repeatedly fell down in the aisle as he tried to approach the platform. It sounded weird. What was the purpose of it? It all seemed very circus-like; it also seemed to demean human dignity, and I questioned whether this was a way God would act.

But when I finally went to a Kathryn Kuhlman meeting, I was struck by the effect of slaying in the Spirit (as she called it) upon the crowd: It led them to glorify God's power. Rather than demeaning people, it seemed as if a real blessing was being imparted, a blessing so powerful that people's bodies were not able to contain it.

Too, I had a chance to talk to several people who had actually been slain in the Spirit. They reported that they felt as light as a feather when they fell; then, during the period when they lay on the floor, they experienced great peace and a sense of God's presence. That softened me up a bit; maybe being slain was worthwhile if it brought a real interior blessing and was not merely a flashy gimmick that some evangelists used to excite the crowd.

So, when someone spotted me in the crowd and an usher brought me up onto the platform, I welcomed the opportunity to be prayed for by Miss Kuhlman. If Jesus wanted to bless me in some deep interior way, I didn't want to resist; I wanted to receive God's blessing, however it might come.

As Kathryn approached me I stood determined not to fight it, whatever it was. A "catcher" stood behind me while several thousand people watched. I felt the gentle pressure of Kathryn's hand on my forehead. I had to make a decision; if I didn't take a step backward, her hand's pressure would push me off-balance and I would fall. But, I thought to myself, I don't want to resist in any way if this is from God.

So I didn't step back and, sure enough, I fell—all six feet four inches of me. The crowd made a noise, a combination of surprise and delight at seeing a priest in a Roman collar topple over on the stage.

Then I quickly scrambled to my feet, not sure that I hadn't been pushed. Again Kathryn prayed; again I felt pressure on my forehead that I did not resist. Once more I fell.

It was confusing. Others, I knew, had experienced something remarkable. But if I had only my own experience to go on, I would have judged that nothing in particular had happened—that I might simply have been pushed off-balance. I didn't know what to make of it.

In time, though, and almost imperceptibly, I began to see it happen *right in front of me as I prayed for others. At first it happened only when I was helping someone else pray. I remember, for instance (in 1971 I think it was), praying with the Rev. Tommy Tyson for an older man seated on a chair. This man acted as though he had fallen asleep and almost fell off that chair. I remember being surprised that Tommy was not surprised! Nor did he appear worried that the man might have suffered a heart attack.*

Aimee Semple McPherson

"A perfect gospel. A complete gospel for body, for soul, for spirit."

Aimee Elizabeth Kennedy (1890–1944) was born in Ontario, Canada. She was raised in the home of Christian parents, her Father a Methodist and her mother a member of the Salvation Army. She was converted in 1908 under the ministry of a visiting Irish evangelist, Robert Semple, whom she soon married. In 1909 Aimee visited the Chicago church of William H. Durham, who ordained her to the ministry. She and her husband then served for a short time as missionaries to China, a ministry that was cut short when Robert died of malaria in 1910.

After Robert's death Aimee returned to the U.S. She ministered in New York and Chicago. While in New York, she married Harold McPherson, and the two ministered together in Canada and the U.S. before separating and divorcing in 1921. In 1919 Aimee was ordained by the Assemblies of God as an "evangelist," but left the denomination in 1922. In the next few years she was ordained also by the Methodist Episcopal Church in Philadelphia and a local Baptist church in San Jose, California.

By 1922, her ministry had become so famous that she filled the largest tents and auditoriums in the nation with people who called her "Sister" and flocked to hear her preach and perform miracles of healing and deliverance. She also decided to build a massive church in Los Angeles, which she named "Angelus Temple." Seating no less than 5,300 persons, it became the nation's first "megachurch," with over 25,000 members at its height. Here she packed the building regularly as she ministered some twenty times per week. She also often wrote and produced her own Christian dramas and cantatas.

The inspiration for a new denomination called the International Church of the Foursquare Gospel came to her in 1922 while preaching on Ezekiel 1:4-10 under a tent in Oakland, California. In 1927, she incorporated her evangelistic and ecclesiastical work under that name. Today the Foursquare Church has missions in some hundred nations and is one of the fastest growing church bodies in the world.

The following excerpt is from Aimee's sermon in Oakland, where she discovered the name for her church. It also illustrates the florid rhetoric for which she was famous.

My soul was awed. My heart athrill. The blazing glory of that heavenly vision seemed to fill and permeate not only the tabernacle but the whole earth.

In the clouds of heaven—which folded and unfolded in fiery glory—Ezekiel had beheld that Being, whose glory no mortal can describe. As he gazed upon that marvelous revelation of the

Omnipotent One he perceived four faces. The faces—those of a man, a lion, an ox, and an eagle. These four faces we likened unto the four phases of the gospel of Jesus Christ.

In the face of the Man we beheld that of the Man of Sorrows and acquainted with grief, dying on the tree.

In the face of the Lion we beheld that of the mighty Baptizer with the Holy Ghost and fire.

The face of the Ox typified the Great burden Bearer, who himself took our infirmities and carried our sicknesses, which in his boundless love and divine provision had met our every need.

In the face of the Eagle we saw reflected soul-enrapturing visions of the coming King, whose pinions soon would cleave the shining heavens, whose silvery voice would set the milky way to echoing as he came to catch his waiting bride away.

A perfect gospel. A complete gospel for body, for soul, for spirit, and for eternity. A gospel that faces squarely in every direction.

As the wonder, the power, the majesty of it cascaded over the battlements of glory, filling, flooding, and enveloping my very being, the fingers of the Spirit swept the aeolian harp strings of my heart and evoked a grand and wondrous melody like the sound of a great amen. It was as if the lost chord was found again! In my soul was born a harmony that was struck and sustained upon four, full, quivering strings, and from it were plucked the words that sprang up and leaped into being— the "Foursquare Gospel."

The whole tent was enveloped, was aquiver! 'Twas as though every soul was brought into harmony with celestial music. I stood there still and listened, gripping my pulpit, shaking with wonder and with joy. Then I exclaimed, "Why—why it's the F-o-u-r-s-q-u-a-r-e G-o-s-p-e-l." The words burst forth from the white heat of my heart.

Instantly the Spirit bore witness! Waves, billows, oceans of praise *rocked the audience. Borne aloft upon the winds of a Holy Ghost revival, the melody evoked that day has been carried round the world. The term "Foursquare Gospel" which the Lord gave me that day, as vividly and fittingly distinguishing the message which he had given me to preach, has become a household word throughout the earth!*

❧

Asa Mahan

"The dispensation of the Spirit"

Asa Mahan (1800–1889) was born in Mt. Vernon, New York, and graduated from Andover Theological Seminary. He was an active Congregationalist pastor before becoming president of the new Oberlin College in Ohio in 1835. Here he worked for fifteen years with the famous evangelist Charles G. Finney. Oberlin is famous for being the first college in America to admit women as well as African-American students.

Under Mahan and Finney, the faculty soon developed what became known as the "Oberlin Theology," which combined Arminian and perfectionist views that caused consternation among the strict Calvinists of the day. In 1839, Mahan published the *Scripture Doctrine of Christian Perfection,* a book that reflected Wesleyan positions on entire sanctification as a second work of grace.

In 1870, Mahan republished the book with a new title, *The Baptism of the Holy Ghost,* with a new theology of the "second blessing." Here he uses Holy Spirit texts from the book of Acts to define the sanctification experience as a "baptism of the Holy Spirit" that brings an endowment of power for service. The following passage from the preface of the book lays a doctrinal groundwork for the rise of Pentecostalism in the twentieth century, with its teaching on a subsequent baptism in the Holy Spirit experience separate from and subsequent to conversion.

The same holds true of all believers, the least as well as the greatest, under the present dispensation, the dispensation of the Spirit. As with the apostles and their associates, so with every believer in Jesus. After inducing "repentance toward God, and faith toward our Lord Jesus Christ," the Spirit abides with and works in him, as he did in them prior to the Pentecost, and for the one purpose, to perfect his love and obedience and inward preparation, that "the Holy Ghost may fall on him as he did on them at the beginning."

If the convert stops short of this great consummation, and if he does this especially under the belief that he did receive "the baptism of the Holy Ghost" in conversion, and that, consequently, nothing remains for him but a gradual increase of what he then received, he will almost inevitably remain through life in the darkness and weakness of the old, instead of going forth to his life work under "the enduements of power," spiritual illuminations, transforming visions of the divine glory, "fellowships with the Father and with his Son Jesus Christ," and "assurances of faith," "assurances of hope," and "assurances of understanding," peculiar to the New Dispensation.

Here this great doctrine is met by the counter one, that every newborn soul does receive the promised "baptism of the Holy Ghost," and all accompanying enlightenments and "enduements of power," at the time of his conversion. In confirmation of this doctrine such passages are adduced as those which affirm that the bodies of all believers "are the temples of the Holy Ghost," "that all have been baptized into one body," and that "if any man have not the Spirit of Christ, he is none of his."

All this, we teach, is true of every convert now, and has been true of every converted person since the Fall. The Holy Ghost had given the disciples "repentance unto life," and "was with them" as a sanctifying presence, had made their bodies his temple, and had "baptized them into one body," prior to the Pentecost. They must have had "the Spirit of Christ, or they could not have been his."

Yet, in the New Testament sense of the words, "the Holy Ghost was not given," and they were not "baptized with the Holy Ghost," until "the Pentecost had fully come." So [also] of all converts in this dispensation. They "have the Spirit of Christ," "the Spirit is with them," and their bodies, as those of all the holy have ever been, are "his temple."

This was true, and must have been true, of all the converts in Samaria before Peter and John came there. Yet "the Holy Ghost had not fallen upon one of them." How any person can contemplate the revealed results of "the baptism of the Holy Ghost," and then affirm, in the presence of palpable facts, that every such convert has received "the enduements of power" included in "the promise of the Spirit," is a mystery of mysteries to us.

Patti Gallagher Mansfield

"All of a sudden I became filled with the Holy Spirit."

The Catholic charismatic renewal began in a prayer retreat
conducted in February 1967 by two professors on the theology
faculty of Duquesne University in Pittsburgh, Pennsylvania.
They were Ralph Keiffer and Bill Storey, who served as advi-
sors for a student prayer group known as *Chi Rho*. They gathered in a retreat center outside of Pittsburgh known as "The
Ark and the Dove." The required readings for the twenty-five
students who gathered at the retreat was Dave Wilkerson's
The Cross and the Switchblade, John Sherrill's *They Speak With
Other Tongues,* and the first four chapters of the Acts of the
Apostles.

The best account of this historic gathering was written by
Patti Gallagher (Mansfield), one of the students in the meeting. This is her firsthand account of the first Catholic charismatic prayer meeting that took place on February 17, 1967.

*In the meantime, the Lord had other plans for us. That night we
had scheduled a party, but nobody seemed to be ready for light talking
or dancing. I wandered up to chapel without really knowing why, but
as soon as I knelt down I began to tremble.*

*Suddenly I didn't want to leave. I remember reasoning with myself
that Christ is in other people and that I should go down with them and
not expect to spend my whole life in a chapel. There were three other*

students with me when all of a sudden I became filled with the Holy Spirit and realized that "God is real."

I started laughing and crying at the same time, because not only did I know that he is real, but that he loves us. And this love that he has is almost foolish because we're so unworthy and yet he continues to freely give us his grace. I wanted to share this wonderful knowledge and joy with the others, but they seemed so detached.

For a moment I thought it might just be a beautiful dream. The next thing I knew I was prostrate before the altar and filled with the peace of Christ.

I experienced what it means "to dwell in his love." In coming home to the Father who made me I felt more complete and free than ever before. I knew I was unworthy and did not have enough faith, and yet I was begging him to stay and never leave me.

As much as I wanted to remain there with him, I knew, just as the apostles after Pentecost, that I must share this with others. If I could experience the love and power of God in this way, anyone could.

That night the Lord brought the whole group into the chapel. I found my prayers pouring forth that the others might come to know him, too. My former shyness about praying aloud was completely gone as the Holy Spirit spoke through me.

The professors then laid hands on some of the students, but most of us received the "baptism in the Spirit" while kneeling before the Blessed Sacrament in prayer. Some of us started speaking in tongues, while others received gifts of discernment, prophecy, and wisdom. But the most important gift was the fruit of love which bound the whole community together. In the Lord's Spirit we found a unity we had long tried to achieve on our own.

∾

Dwight L. Moody

"I had to ask him to stay his hand."

Dwight Lyman Moody (1837–99) was born in Northfield, Massachussetts. The sixth child in a poor family of nine children, as a young man he was consumed with a desire to strike it rich as a businessman. Although he never went beyond the sixth grade in school he was possessed with a shrewd native intelligence. At the age of seventeen he left for Boston, where he reportedly hoped to gain a fortune of some $100,000. He soon was very successful in the shoe business and was well on his way to financial success.

Moody's religious interests date from an encounter with a Sunday school teacher who led him to Christ in his store. Because of his lack of education, he felt unqualified to preach, so he began to tell young boys about Jesus and soon led a large group of them to church. Many were converted.

His success in witnessing eventually led him to retire from business and embark on a pastoral and evangelistic ministry that eventually filled the largest arenas in America and Britain. In 1864 he founded a church in Chicago that now bears the name Moody Memorial Church. In an amazing lifetime, Moody founded three schools, preached to about 1,000,000 people in person, and reshaped Victorian Christianity.

In 1871, while pastoring in Chicago, Moody noticed two

women who sat near the front of the church praying for him as he preached. They were Free Methodist women from the Holiness tradition. They told Moody that he needed to be baptized with the Holy Spirit. Soon Moody became a seeker for such a baptism. The following testimony tells the story of Moody's experience as reported by James Gilchrist Lawson.

Moody continued to hunger for a deepening of his own spiritual life and experience. He had been greatly used of God, but felt that there were greater things in store for him. The year 1871 was a critical one with him. He realized more and more how little he was fitted by personal acquirements for his work, and how much he needed to be qualified for service by the Holy Spirit's power.

This realization was deepened by conversations he had with two ladies who sat on the front pew in his church. He could see by the expression of their faces that they were praying. At the close of the service they would say to him, "We have been praying for you."

"Why don't you pray for the people?" Mr. Moody would ask.

"Because you need the power of the Spirit," was the reply.

"I need the power! Why," he said, in relating the incident afterwards, "I thought I had the power. I had the largest congregation in Chicago, and there were many conversions. I was in a sense satisfied.

"But right along those two godly women kept praying for me, and their earnest talk about anointing for special service set me thinking. I asked them to come and talk with me, and they poured out their hearts in prayer that I might receive the filling of the Holy Spirit. There came a great hunger into my soul. I did not know what it was.

"I began to cry out as I never did before. I really felt that I did not want to live if I could not have this power for service."

"While Mr. Moody was in this mental and spiritual condition," says his son, "Chicago was laid in ashes. The great fire swept out of

existence both Farwell Hall and Illinois Street Church. On Sunday night after the meeting, as Mr. Moody went homeward, he saw the glare of flames, and knew it meant ruin to Chicago. About one o'clock Farwell Hall was burned; and soon his church went down. Everything was scattered."

Mr. Moody went East to New York City to collect funds for the sufferers from the Chicago fire, but his heart and soul were crying out for the power from on high. "My heart was not in the work of begging," says he. "I could not appeal. I was crying all the time that God would fill me with his Spirit.

"Well, one day, in the city of New York—oh, what a day!—I cannot describe it; I seldom refer to it; it is almost too sacred an experience to name. Paul had such an experience of which he never spoke for fourteen years. I can only say that God revealed himself to me, and I had such an experience of his love that I had to ask him to stay his hand.

"I went to preaching again. The sermons were not different; I did not present any new truths, and yet hundreds were converted. I would not now be placed back where I was before that blessed experience if you should give me all the world—it would be as the small dust of the balance."

Jennie Moore

"I sang under the power of the Spirit in many languages."

Jennie Evans Moore (1883–1936), who worked as a maid, lived across the street from the Bonnie Brae home of Richard

Asberry, where William J. Seymour held services before the opening of the Azusa Street Mission in 1906. Attending Seymour's first services on Bonnie Brae, Moore was the first woman to speak in tongues in Los Angeles, even before Seymour himself. She also sang in tongues and, although she had no prior training, played the piano under the inspiration of the Spirit. She became one of the earliest pentecostal evangelists by spreading the word of the baptism in the Holy Spirit and the tongues evidence in several Los Angeles churches.

When Seymour opened services on Azusa Street in April 1906, Moore was there as a capable helper, leading singing and serving as an altar worker. In 1907 and 1908, she traveled with two other women holding services in Los Angeles and Chicago with William Durham.

In May 1908 she married William J. Seymour and served at his side during the rest of his ministry. When Seymour died in 1922, Jennie served as pastor of the Azusa Street Mission, which by then was a small black pentecostal congregation. She died in 1936.

Throughout the years after 1906, Moore often sang in tongues, which at Azusa Street was called "the heavenly choir." The following testimony gives her account of singing in tongues for the first time on Bonnie Brae Street on April 9, 1906.

For years before this wonderful experience came to us, we as a family, were seeking to know the fullness of God, and he was filling us with his presence until we could hardly contain the power. I had never seen a vision in my life, but one day as we prayed there passed before me three white cards, each with two names thereon, and but for fear I could have given them, as I saw every letter distinctly.

On April 9, 1906, I was praising the Lord from the depths of my heart at home, and when the evening came and we attended the meeting the power of God fell and I was baptized in the Holy Ghost and fire, with the evidence of speaking in tongues. During the day I had told the Father that although I wanted to sing under the power I was willing to do whatever he willed, and at the meeting when the power came on me I was reminded of the three cards which had passed me in the vision months ago.

As I thought thereon and looked to God, it seemed as if a vessel broke within me and water surged up through my being, which when it reached my mouth came out in a torrent of speech in the languages which God had given me. I remembered the names on the cards: French, Spanish, Latin, Greek, Hebrew, Hindustani, and as the message came with power, so quick that but few words would have been recognized, interpretation of each message followed in English, the name of the language would come to me.

I sang under the power of the Spirit in many languages, the interpretation both words and music which I had never before heard, and in the home where the meeting was being held, the Spirit led me to the piano, where I played and sang under inspiration, although I had not learned to play. In these ways God is continuing to use me to his glory ever since that wonderful day and I praise him for the privilege of being a witness for him under the Holy Ghost's power.

❧

Dan T. Muse

"The men at the shop hardly knew what to think."

Daniel Thomas Muse (1882–1950) was born in Boonesboro, Mississippi, and as a youngster took an interest in the printing business. He also loved to hunt, fish, and take part in other activities that boys his age enjoyed. An early inclination to spiritual matters began when his grandfather, a Baptist preacher, called young Dan over on his deathbed, laid his hands on him, and prayed that God would use him to preach the gospel. He later settled down, married, and had three children, but still ran from the call of God that he had felt ever since the episode with his grandfather years before.

Soon after attending a revival service in a Baptist church, Muse went home and sought God for his salvation. Upon receiving the joy and peace of Christ, he then led his wife to Christ. Muse was growing in his faith and had begun hearing about what some were calling the "baptism in the Holy Spirit." He was anxious to obtain this deeper connection with God for himself, so on May 1, 1913, Muse attended his first pentecostal worship service.

I went to the mission and was the first person in the altar to seek the baptism of the Spirit. I had never witnessed or heard anyone receiving the baptism. One brother received the experience that night and I edged over to touch his body while he was talking in tongues.

Sunday, May 11, 1913, at the altar I promised God that I would go anywhere and tell the good news if he would only fill me with the Holy Ghost. Monday night I attended a meeting of the men of the church I had been attending and the superintendent of education was to address the body. Here I had the opportunity of testifying and informing the people I was definitely seeking the baptism of the Holy Ghost as was received on the day of Pentecost.

The last thing hurled at me was "Holiness preachers never amount to anything." The next night I was filled with the Holy Ghost (May 13, 1913), Jim Campbell and others at my side....

I was completely in the hands of the living God. There was never anything in my life sweeter than to feel myself completely in the power of God—I felt so good when the Spirit commenced to use my tongue that I guess I shouted (I sure felt like it). I was happier than I ever was before in my life and the folks said I woke up the neighborhood.

For about three and one half hours Tuesday night the Spirit witnessed through me. (Just a minute. Understand that when the Spirit is using you, you have complete control of all your faculties except your tongue, and your body when the Lord wants to shake you up a little, and you seem drunk sometimes as on the day of Pentecost. You can communicate to people by writing your messages to them and them talking to you.) I don't know what language the Spirit used in speaking through me; it was enough for me to know that the Holy Ghost was talking.

You might well think a man would be hoarse after shouting and talking for three and a half hours, but the Lord keeps you from getting hoarse.... Well, to hasten on. Wednesday I could speak English most all day but Thursday the Holy Ghost took charge of my tongue again and most every time I opened my mouth—bless God—the Holy Ghost spake.

The men at the shop hardly knew what to think. I could hear what they said and could write and go ahead with my work just the same as ever, but there was one other young man that had already been baptized with the Holy Ghost working with me, so he explained to them what the glad news was.

∽

David Wesley Myland

"I was singing the 'latter rain' song in 'tongues.'"

David Wesley Myland (1858–1943) was born in Ontario, Canada, and raised in the Methodist Episcopal Church. Because of his interest in healing, he was drawn to the Holiness movement. By 1900 he had identified with the Christian and Missionary Alliance and the World's Faith Missionary Association, Holiness groups that emphasized second blessing sanctification as a "baptism in the Holy Spirit" without the expectation of tongues. Learning of the pentecostal outpouring at Azusa Street in 1906, he was drawn to seek a baptism in the Holy Spirit with the "Bible evidence" of speaking in tongues.

In October of 1906, while on a preaching mission in Akron, Ohio, he "was earnestly seeking Pentecost." His search ended on November 3, 1906, when he was transported to heaven in a vision, where he finally received his coveted pentecostal experience.

In 1910, Myland published his testimony in *The Latter Rain Covenant,* one of the earliest theological books defending the new pentecostal movement. This book was unique in that Myland included the annual rainfall patterns in Palestine in order to prove that not only were spiritual rains falling, but also increasing physical rain in the Holy Land. This information was gathered to strengthen the claims that the pentecostal revival was indeed the "latter rain" that was promised in Joel 2:23.

Myland's pentecostal testimony tells of singing in tongues as evidence of the baptism in the Holy Spirit, a not-uncommon claim in the early days. What was different in Myland's case was that his experience happened while he was singing in a heavenly choir led by Jesus himself:

In that hour I saw the Lord Jesus. He wasn't down here exactly as Daniel saw him, but away up in glory and in the midst of a great multitude. A great orchestra was before me and a great chorus of singers, and they were singing wonderful music.

I could see him on a glorious pedestal with a beautiful baton that looked like gold and pearl, beating time, and as I looked upon him I wished he would turn around so I could see his face. Presently, as they seemed to come to a pause in the singing at the end of a strain, he turned around so gracefully to me, and looked at me and said, "Well, my child, what would you like to have?"

And I said, "Oh, Lord, I would like to join your choir," and then I seemed to tremble at what I had said: Join that choir!

He turned and looked toward the choir and then at me and said, "My child, you may," and then all the strength left me.

I said, "Well, I can't now, I wouldn't dare." But he made a motion to me with his baton, and it seemed I was lifted right up and was set down in the choir. I began to sing with them a little, and what do you suppose? I was singing the "latter rain" song in "tongues," which I afterwards interpreted and wrote into English.

They all seemed to join in with me, and after it was all over they sang another great chorus. I listened, and the great Leader, my glorified Christ, motioned to me and I sat down, and I thought, Oh, what singing! The old Ohio Quartette never could sing like that, and I found myself singing also. The glory died away and I came to myself singing in "tongues."

It passed away, and immediately I began to reach for my Bible. I took out a piece of blank paper and began to write with my left hand, tried to write with my pencil between the first and second finger. I could not get along very fast and involuntarily took it over into my right hand, the hand that had been so badly swollen, and I found I was healed; the sores were there, but I was healed. There wasn't a particle of pain or stiffness, and I wrote the words of the "Latter Rain Song," word for word, as fast as I could write, never changed a word, wrote the melody, tried it on the piano, and found it a beautiful melody.

༒

Agnes Ozman

"I wanted the promise of the Father more than I wanted food or sleep."

Agnes Nevada Ozman (1870–1937) was born in Albany, Wisconsin, one of six children in a poor farming family. Her parents taught their children to work hard, be kind to others, and love the Lord. Agnes gave her heart to the Lord as an early child. As she later recalled, "At family prayer I learned to bring my sins to Jesus and to know he forgave me. I do not remember when I was first forgiven of my sins. I thank God for the call of God to the children's hearts."

Agnes always had a love for the Lord, and as she grew, she began to be involved in various mission projects. During her early years she became deeply involved with the Holiness movement and began a healing ministry. She later felt a desire to attend Bible School so she could be better prepared for future service.

One of the schools Agnes attended was Charles Parham's Bethel Bible College in Topeka, Kansas. Surely no one realized that God would use this small, unmarried Wisconsin woman from such humble beginnings to be his catalyst for spreading the latter-day outpouring of the Holy Spirit, which was soon to cover all the earth.

Agnes believed intently the preaching of Charles Parham, who taught that God wanted to baptize his people in the Holy Spirit for holiness and power. She and several other girls in the school had begun praying for God to pour out his Spirit upon them as in the days of the New Testament church.

J. Roswell Flower, a pioneer leader in the Assemblies of God, said that Agnes' experience of baptism in the Holy Spirit with the accompanying sign of speaking in tongues "made the pentecostal movement of the twentieth century." This event in fact occurred on January 1, 1901, the very first day of the twentieth century. The following excerpts of her testimony, published in her 1921 autobiography, offer her recollection of what some have called "the touch felt around the world."

It was proclaimed and preached that God had a mighty outpouring and baptism of the Holy Ghost and power for his people everywhere and that it was our privilege to have it fulfilled in us here and now. At first, and for a time, I held to the experiences I had had in joy, answers to prayer and seeing the sick healed as the baptism of the Spirit. Soon, however, I was convinced of a need within. For about three weeks my heart became hungry for the baptism of the Holy Ghost. I wanted the promise of the Father more than I wanted food or sleep....

As the last of the year (1900) drew near some friends came from Kansas City to spend a few days with us during the holidays. On watch night a blessed service was held praying and blessing God as the New Year 1901, came in. During the day the presence and power of the Lord was present in a marked way, giving refreshing and stirring our hearts to wait still upon him for greater things. And God blessed us very much and the spirit of prayer was upon us in the evening....

On New Year's night, January 1, 1901, near eleven o'clock, I asked that prayer be offered for me and hands laid on me to fulfill all Scripture, that I might receive the baptism which my whole heart longed to have. There as I was praying I remembered in the Bible hands were laid on believers as on me and prayer was offered for me. I asked Bro. Parham to pray and to lay hands on me that I might receive the baptism of the Holy Ghost, and as he laid his hands upon my head, I began to talk in tongues and had great joy and was filled with the glory.

Bless him! I talked several languages for it was manifested when a dialect was spoken. Glory to God. I had the added joy and glory my heart longed for and a depth of the presence of the Lord within I never knew before.

After this fulfillment of promise as in Acts 19:1-6, others in the school became hungry for this outpouring and three days after the baptism of the Holy Ghost came in me, he was received by twelve others;

each one spoke in tongues. Some had the interpretation also, and when the language was spoken it was translated into English and all was edifying.

I did not know that I would talk in tongues when I received the baptism, but as soon as I received on that night, I spoke in tongues. I knew that I had received the promise of the Father, fulfilled. Blessed be God! There came such a joy and fullness of the presence of the Lord in me. I never knew such a presence before.

In the morning of the 2nd of January different ones asked me about the outpouring I had received the night before. God poured out his Spirit upon me so mightily and so wonderfully, and when I began to talk I spoke in tongues. I motioned for paper and pencil, and when I started to write, I did not write in English, but made characters in another language.

Afterwards I opened my Bible in Acts and read about the experiences God gave them and how he had this same mighty outpouring for us today. This was the fulfillment of the promise for which we had been praying.

ॐ

Charles Parham

"A glory fell over me and I began to worship God in the Swedish tongue."

In many ways Charles Fox Parham (1873–1929) was the father of the modern pentecostal movement. The first case of speaking in tongues in the twentieth century occurred under his ministry as he laid hands on Agnes Ozman. William Seymour, one of Parham's students, later pastored the Azusa Street Mission where the great revival broke out in 1906. Parham also helped develop and refine the systematic theology of the young renewal movement. He will always be remembered as one of the great early pioneer pentecostal leaders.

Parham was born in Muscatine, Iowa, and was very sickly as a child, suffering from constant bouts of rheumatic fever as well as what was probably encephalitis. His growth was also stunted. His mother was deeply religious and no doubt had a great influence on young Charles.

Shortly after her death in 1885, her teenage son gave his heart to Christ. Soon after his conversion he began to feel the call to preach. He was very impressed with the Holiness preaching and its emphasis on the power of the Spirit that was popular at the time. He soon began to find himself longing for a deeper experience with the Holy Spirit so he could do more for the kingdom of God.

The following is Parham's testimony of how he received the baptism in the Holy Spirit two nights after Agnes Ozman's tongues experience had electrified the Bethel Bible School campus.

On the night of January 3rd, I preached at the Free Methodist Church in the City of Topeka, telling them what had already happened, and that I expected upon returning the entire school to be baptized in the Holy Spirit. On returning to the school with one of the students, we ascended to the second floor, and passing down along the corridor in the upper room, heard most wonderful sounds. The door was slightly ajar, the room was lit with only coal oil lamps. As I pushed open the door I found the room was filled with a sheen of white light above the brightness of the lamps.

Twelve ministers of different denominations, who were in the school, were filled with the Holy Spirit and spoke with other tongues. Some were sitting, some still kneeling, others standing with hands upraised. Here was no violent physical manifestation, though some trembled under the power of the glory that filled them.

Sister Stanley, an elderly lady, came across the room as I entered, telling me that just before I entered tongues of fire were sitting above their heads.

When I beheld the evidence of the restoration of pentecostal power, my heart was melted in gratitude to God for what my eyes had seen. For years I had suffered terrible persecutions for preaching holiness and healing and the soon coming of the Lord. I fell to my knees behind a table unnoticed by those upon whom the power of pentecost had fallen to pour out my heart to God in thanksgiving. All at once they began to sing, "Jesus, Lover of My Soul" in at least six different languages, carrying the different parts but with a more angelic voice than I had ever listened to in all my life.

After praising God for some time, I asked him for the same blessing. He distinctly made it clear to me that he raised me up and trained me to declare this mighty truth to the world, and if I was willing to stand for it, with all the persecutions, hardships, trials, slander, scandal that it would entail, he would give me the blessing. And I said, "Lord, I will, if you will just give me this blessing." Right then there came a slight twist in my throat, a glory fell over me, and I began to worship God in the Swedish tongue, which later changed to other languages and continued so until the morning.

❧

Jonathan Paul

"Since then I had to speak and sing in tongues every day."

Jonathan Alexander Benjamin Paul (1853–1931) was born in Gartz, East Germany. As the son of a Lutheran pastor, he was baptized on July 8. At this event his father dedicated him to the Lord to be a preacher of the gospel. At an early age Jonathan made a decision to follow Christ. He started to study theology in 1872 in Greifswald. In 1880 he was called to serve in Nörenberg and became pastor in Ravenstein in 1889.

At this time, Paul came into contact with the Holiness movement and began to seek an experience of entire sanctification. After coming under spiritual conviction about smoking, he surrendered his life to the Lord in June 1890 and reported the following experience.

When I woke up the next morning, I arose as a different person. Things that had previously attracted me, lost all their attraction. In the preceding days I enjoyed smoking a cigar. Smoking, however, now did not appeal to me at all. I could not even understand that I had once been attracted to it ... I received sanctification—Christ was in me.

In 1907, Paul heard about the pentecostal movement through the influence of Thomas Ball Barratt, a Methodist leader in Norway who was introducing pentecostalism to Europe at the time. After a visit to Barratt's services in Christiana (Oslo), in 1907, Paul received a vivid baptism in the

Holy Spirit with unusual manifestations of speaking and singing in tongues. Of his baptism in the Holy Spirit, he wrote:

On September 15 the power of the Lord came over me during the morning gathering. Throughout the whole day I could experience the power of the Lord in my body, whenever I came into the meeting of believers. Although I was still able to take part in the meals and activities of everyday life, I had the inner desire to experience the blessing I was longing for. I experienced such a joy, that I considered myself one of the happiest people.

During the evening we (a group of seven brothers) had another prayer meeting. At 11 o'clock those among us who were working the next morning left. Besides me two other brothers stayed (one of them was pastor Horst).

As we started praying again, I experienced that my mouth was moving, and I realized that I needed the gift to bring sound to the movement of my lips. I looked up to the Lord to give it to me and soon afterwards had the desire to start speaking. A wonderful language came forth with sounds I had never spoken before. According to the sounds, it seemed like Chinese.

Then emerged a new language with completely different sounds. As we had in these days a missions conference for China and for the South Sea, I had the impression that this might have been the language of the South Sea. I do not know how long I spoke like this. It must have been for quite a few minutes.

I then had to praise and worship God in German. I experienced how my body was shaken by a mighty power—this was, however, not painful or uncomfortable at all. On the contrary, a still rest reigned in me, while my body, the earthly vessel, trembled under the power and majesty of the Lord. I could not do anything else, but crying out repeatedly: "O Jesus, how beautiful you are!"

In a short time, Paul experienced singing in the Spirit, which came to him in perfect verses with rhyming phrases. Of these experiences he wrote:

It was the evening of September 20. I already had to speak in tongues during the morning and now, as I was busy writing, I had the urge to speak in tongues again. I had the desire to speak and to sing in tongues.

This is something extraordinarily wonderful; not only the words were given to me in tongues, but also the melody and the beat. Since then I had to speak and sing in tongues every day. New songs with completely different melodies and words continually come to me. These are so many—up to the time I am writing now, I must have sung more than two hundred different verses.

I mention this as a testimony. Songs must abound in heaven! It seems as if the songs I sing belong to at least three different languages. I do not know, however, what I sing, because the Lord has not given me the gift of interpretation yet.

∾

Pope Paul VI

"A blessing for the Church and for the world."

The Catholic charismatic renewal began in 1967 during the reign of Pope Paul VI (1897–1978). For several years various groups of bishops gave cautious approval to the movement without any official word from the Vatican. Catholic charismatic leaders were aware that the renewal could be accepted or rejected by the Pope, and everyone was anxious to hear his first official pronouncement.

This first official papal pronouncement concerning the renewal came in a Mass on Pentecost Sunday, May 19, 1975, in St. Peter's Basilica, where 10,000 charismatics had gathered for their third international conference. For several days conference sessions were conducted in the area of the catacombs. In the climactic session, Cardinal Leon Joseph Suenens of Belgium joined with the Pope to celebrate the Pentecost Mass.

The following are excerpts from Pope Paul's official address and an informal talk in Italian that he gave extemporaneously to the waiting charismatics:

Dear Sons and Daughters,

In this holy year you have chosen the city of Rome for your third international congress.

You have asked us to meet you today and to speak to you: in so doing you wished to show your attachment to the Church instituted by Jesus Christ and to everything that this See of Peter represents for you. This concern to take your place clearly in the Church is a genuine sign of the action of the Holy Spirit. For God became Man in Christ Jesus, of whom the Church is the Mystical Body, and it is in her that the Spirit of Christ was communicated on the day of Pentecost, when he descended on the apostles gathered in the "upper room," "devoting themselves to prayer," with "Mary the mother of Jesus."

As we said in the presence of some of you last October, the Church and world need more than ever that "the miracle of Pentecost should be continued in history." In fact, modern man, intoxicated by his conquests, has ended up by imagining, according to the expression used in the last Council, he is "an end unto himself, the sole artisan and

131

creator of his own history." Alas! To how many, even of those who continue by tradition, to profess his existence, and out of duty, to pay him worship, has God become a stranger in our lives?

In the middle of the talk, the Pope then made the statement that approved the Catholic charismatic renewal at the highest possible level:

How then could this "spiritual renewal" be other than a blessing for the Church and for the world? And in this case, how could we fail to take all means in order that it should remain so?

After reading the official text, the Pope addressed in Italian the 10,000 people in St. Peter's, both charismatics and many others in attendance:

Very dear ones: it is permissible to add a few words in Italian, in fact, two messages. One is for those of you who are here with the charismatic pilgrimage. The other is for those pilgrims who are present by chance at this great assembly.

First, for you: Reflect on the two-part name by which you are designated, "spiritual renewal." Where the Spirit is concerned we are immediately alert, immediately happy to welcome the coming of the Holy Spirit. More than that, we invite him, we pray to him, we desire nothing more than that Christians, believing people, should experience an awareness, worship, a greater joy through the Spirit of God among us.

Have we forgotten the Holy Spirit? Certainly not! We want him, we honor him, and we love him, and we invoke him.

You, with your devotion and fervor, you wish to live in the Spirit . . . and this should be where the second part of your name comes in—a renewal. It ought to rejuvenate the world, give it back a spirituality, a soul, religious thought. It ought to reopen its closed lips to prayer and open its mouth to song, to joy, to hymns and to witnessing.

It will be very fortuitous for our times, for our brothers, that there should be a generation, your generation of young people, who shout out to the world the glory and the greatness of the God of Pentecost. In the hymn which we read this morning in the breviary, and which dates back as far as St. Ambrose in the third or fourth century, there is this phrase which is so hard to translate, yet should be very simple: Laeti, *which means "joyfully,"* bibamus, *"let us drink,"* sobriam, *that means "well-defined and well-moderated,"* profusionem spiritus *"the outpouring of the Spirit".* Laeti bibamus sobriam profusionem spiritus. *This could be a formula indicating your program.*

The second message is for those pilgrims present at this great assembly who do not belong to your movement. They should unite themselves with you to celebrate the feast of Pentecost—the spiritual renewal of the world, of our society and of our souls—so that they, too, devout pilgrims to this center of the Catholic faith, might nourish themselves on the enthusiasm and the spiritual energy with which we must live our religion. We will say only this: today, either one lives one's faith with devotion, depth, energy and joy, or that faith will die out.

Lewi Pethrus

"A current of power and sweetness went through my entire being."

A man who helped birth the pentecostal message throughout Scandinavia and Europe first experienced the baptism in the Spirit and didn't even realize it! Petrus Lewi Pethrus (1884–1974) was born in Tunhem, Sweden, the son of a factory worker. He grew up in a Baptist church, where he later became an evangelist.

Years later, as pastor of the Filadelfia Baptist church in Stockholm, Sweden, Pethrus heard about the pentecostal movement that was breaking out in Norway under the Methodist Thomas Ball Barratt. In 1907, he journeyed to Oslo (then known as Christiana), where he became a pentecostal. When he returned to Stockholm, his church also accepted pentecostal teaching and worship.

In 1913 the Swedish Baptist Convention expelled Pethrus and the church from their ranks. Nevertheless, in the years afterwards, the Filadelfia church grew to more than 7,000 members. In 1932 they built a sanctuary that seated more than 4,000 persons, becoming the largest free congregation in Sweden and for many years the largest pentecostal church in the world.

In the following testimony, Pethrus tells about his baptism in the Holy Spirit in 1902 while on a ship "observing the majesty and glory of God's creation." That morning he found himself praising God and soon realized that he was speaking strange words that he had never learned.

We prayed all night until it was time to leave for the boat. All of them accompanied me down to the pier. It was a beautiful morning, just at the dawn of one of the matchless pre-summer mornings of the north. I can still remember the tender love and the well wishes of these newfound friends, and the impression of the glorious services is just as vivid. In such a frame of mind I boarded the ship.

I was the only passenger from Lillesand. I watched the sailors pull in the gangway and the boat launch out while the little blessed band of believers waved farewell.

With all of this over I remained on deck—alone. Others were sleeping in their cabins. The seamen who had taken care of the gangway dis-appeared, and I could continue the prayer I had been engaged in through the night. While I stood there by the railing and prayed, the sun rose up out of the ocean. I have always been impressed by the majesty and beauty of nature, but this time I experienced something altogether new. The experiences of this last night, my contact with God through prayer, and the wonderful scenery of nature before me—all seemed to overwhelm me.

Tears streamed down my cheeks while I was overflowing with joy. A current of power and sweetness went through my entire being, and I spoke strange words which surprised me a great deal. In this condition I continued to experience the power of God, and remained on deck for a long time until the boat was way out at sea before I began to settle down for the long voyage.

It was not until the pentecostal revival broke through and Pastor Barratt came to Norway with the message about the baptism in the Spirit that I understood what I had experienced on board the ship in 1902 was the baptism in the Holy Ghost accompanied by this sign of tongues.

Later when I saw the manifestations of the Spirit in others, I real-ized that what I experienced in 1902 of the power of God accompanied by speaking in tongues was the baptism in the Holy Spirit. It is not any more remarkable than that.

Many people are hindered from receiving the baptism in the Holy Spirit because they are expecting something which, as far as they are concerned, never will come. They are expecting violent outward man-ifestations, but they are waiting in vain. In my case the power came upon me very unexpectedly when I, for the first time, experienced this power and spoke in tongues.

When I was in Oslo in February of 1907, I prayed for the baptism in the Holy Spirit. I expected then to have a very remarkable experience with great outward manifestations, but they never came. In one way I left Kristiana disappointed, because I had not experienced the physical manifestation of the baptism in the Holy Spirit which I had expected. Nevertheless, in my personal relationship to God and to my environ- ment, wonderful things had transpired which would be of great future importance to my life.

∾

Pandita Ramabai

"Those who have received this powerful baptism for service are growing in power."

Pandita Sarasvti Ramabai (1858–1922) was born in the Gangamula Forest of India. She was raised a strict Hindu, and as a young woman had memorized thousands of verses from the sacred Hindu writings. Her faith, however, could not con- sole her broken heart over the way women were treated in her native land. Women were extremely low in the eyes of society, and if one was unfortunate enough to be born one, the only hope was to pray for a better reincarnation in the next life. Often times widows would burn themselves alive on their hus- band's funeral pyre, because without a husband, a woman was thought useless.

These and other philosophical questions were on the mind of Pandita when she took a trip to England in 1883. While there she was taken in by the love and ministry of the kind sisters of St. Mary's Home. She grew inquisitive about the Christian faith and was amazed to hear of a personal God who loved all people—even women.

The story of Jesus' treatment of the Samaritan woman helped her understand her value and worth in God's eyes. She later accepted Christ and returned to India with a dual passion of helping Indian women and sharing Christ in the home that she started for outcast women and girls.

Later Ramabai founded a girls' school in Mukti, where girls who became Christians were saved from death or lives of degradation. Here a great revival broke out in 1905, where many manifestations took place among the girls. Among them were visible manifestations of fire and speaking in tongues. Later, the pentecostal revival in Chile was influenced by reports of the Indian revival in 1905.

One famous incident occurred when Pandita was sharing from the eighth chapter of the book of John.

In January of 1905, Pandita Ramabai spoke to the Mukti children about the necessity of an awakening and invited those who would do so voluntarily to join her daily to pray toward that end. Seventy girls volunteered, and from time to time, others joined them. When the awakening began, there were 550 of them meeting twice a day.

In June, Pandita Ramabai asked volunteers of the Bible School to leave their secular studies and go out into the surrounding villages to preach the gospel. Thirty young people volunteered, and we were meeting daily to pray in order to be "filled with power" when the revival came.

On June 20th, at 3:30 A.M., the Holy Spirit was poured upon one of these volunteers. The young lady who slept near her awakened when this happened, and seeing her covered with flames, ran through the bedroom, grabbed a bucket of water, and was at the point of throwing it on her when she realized that she was not being consumed.

At first, some of the missionaries thought that the fire poured out upon the children during their time of repentance was necessary for their purification since they had been idol worshippers. But when people who were fully saved and sanctified also received the baptism of the Holy Spirit and fire, those workers began to search the Word of God to see if this experience and this power for service was for them as well.

Fifteen months have now passed since this awakening began. The lives are truly transformed and those that have achieved a complete salvation are walking with God in a life of daily victory, and those who have received this powerful baptism for service are growing in power. The Word of God, confirmed with the example of these lives filled with power for service, have convinced us that this baptism of the Holy Spirit and fire is for all those who are ready to completely put themselves at the disposition of God for his work and his glory.

❧

Kevin Ranaghan

"Many of us received that night the gift of praising God in strange languages."

Kevin (1940–) and Dorothy Ranaghan were two of the earliest leaders of the charismatic renewal in the Roman Catholic Church. In Kevin's 1969 book *Catholic Pentecostals*, he tells about his baptism in the Holy Spirit in the home of Ray

Bullard, the president of the South Bend chapter of the Full Gospel Business Men's Fellowship International (FGBMFI). Bullard was a janitor in a local junior high school, and Ranaghan and his friends were graduate theology students at Notre Dame University.

Despite the huge cultural and theological gap between the Catholic students and the humble pentecostals, the pentecostal event in Bullard's basement helped to spark the incredible Holy Spirit renewal that swept the Notre Dame campus in the months that followed.

On Monday, March 13, another group made up mostly of those who had received the baptism in the Holy Spirit the week before and a few newcomers went to a prayer meeting in the home of Ray and Mable Bullard in nearby Mishawaka. Ray was president of the local South Bend chapter of the Full Gospel Business Men's Fellowship International, an interfaith group of laymen who share the experience of the "baptism in the Holy Spirit." We had heard of this group and thought it good to share our experience with them.

If the pentecostal movement were merely a human fiction, or even a form of religiosity created out of the wills of men, it would have crumbled to dust that evening. Never would we have thought it possible for men and women, so radically different from each other in countless ways, to unite in the love of Christ. Yet, we were united by Christ.

Here we were, a group of Roman Catholics, formed in the spiritual and liturgical traditions of our Church, all university-trained "intellectual types." The people with whom we were meeting were mostly from an evangelical background. They spoke with a scriptural and theological fundamentalism that was very foreign to us. Furthermore, the way they spoke and prayed, the type of hymns they sang—all this was so different that at first it was very disturbing.

139

On the natural level these "cultural" differences were more than enough to keep us far apart from each other. Yet, in spite of these personal differences, we were enabled to come together in common faith in Jesus, in the one experience of his Holy Spirit, to worship our Father together. That was no human achievement. The Holy Spirit simply cut across these cultural barriers to unite us as brothers and sisters in Christ. Many of us received that night the gift of praising God in strange languages.

Another young Catholic student present in Ray Bullard's basement was Bert Ghezzi, who later became an important leader in the Catholic charismatic renewal. In his report he tells of a fateful decision that he said made the renewal possible in the Church.

After a time of praying in tongues, Ghezzi says, the students' pentecostal friends asked them when they would be leaving the Catholic Church and joining up with a pentecostal church:

The question actually left us a little shocked. Our response was that we wouldn't be leaving the Catholic Church, that being baptized in the Holy Spirit was completely compatible with our belief in the Catholic Church. We assured our friends that we had a great respect for them and that we would have fellowship with them, but we would be remaining in the Catholic Church.

I think there's something significant about the fact that those of us who were baptized in the Holy Spirit then would never have thought about abandoning the Roman Catholic Church.

Our pentecostal friends had seen Catholics join pentecostal churches when they were baptized in the Spirit. Because we did not do that, the Catholic charismatic renewal became possible.

Oral Roberts

"You are going to take my healing power to your generation."

The most influential and well-known healing evangelist of the twentieth century is without a doubt Granville Oral Roberts (1918–). A child of poverty, Oral was born in a log cabin home to Ellis and Claudius Roberts in Pontotoc County, Oklahoma. Claudius received a premonition from God that the child she carried was special and destined to be used greatly by God.

It seemed as if that would not happen, however, as Roberts was stricken with tuberculosis at age seventeen and almost died. The year was 1935 when his family took him to hear an evangelist, George W. Moncey, to be prayed over for healing. Before he arrived at the tent, Roberts claimed to hear an audible voice:

God spoke to me ... Audibly! Every fragment of my consciousness tingled and I was in sacred conversation with a divine Presence. His existence was so vibrant that I can only describe him as God.... I was conscious of the car and the presence of others with me, but I was remote from them.... I was alone with God, his words were clear and unmistakable. "Son, I am going to heal you and you are going to take my healing power to your generation."

After his healing, Roberts sent the following letter to the Pentecostal Holiness Advocate, the official organ of his denomination:

I am happy and free because I have just been saved and sanctified. It is so glorious I want everyone to know it. Surely I have a right to be happy....

I have been bedfast for 130 days, and I praise God for it. During this time I have been saved and sanctified. I have had several doctors, medical and chiropractic, but they seem of no avail. It seems that God is the only one that knows my condition. He has been dealing with me for a long time, and I have now awakened to the realization that I must obey him. I feel the call to preach very definitely, but before I recover and enter into the work I must have the abiding Comforter, the Holy Ghost, to comfort me and help me to overcome my infirmities.

Dear readers, if you ever prayed an earnest prayer, please do so for me. The field is so broad, and the workers are few, I feel I must hurry and enter it. As I lie in bed thinking it grieves my heart that so many are unsaved and others are falling away because the cross is so great.

After a total healing from the tuberculosis and his life-long stuttering problem, Roberts threw himself into the work of the ministry. At the young age of eighteen he was ordained into the Pentecostal Holiness church and later served four pastorates. In 1947 Roberts started traveling the country to conduct healing crusades.

Thousands upon thousands were healed at his meetings, and sometimes he would personally pray for over a thousand people a night, laying hands on them and asking God to heal their afflictions. One night in particular stands out. Roberts described the following remarkable scene that took place in a crusade meeting in Jacksonville, Florida, in 1951:

The miracle started and all of a sudden I cried out that my right hand was like it was on fire. My hand was burning like you were sticking it with a thousand pins....

Suddenly I jumped to my feet. I didn't say anything and the crowd jumped up and here they came and completely engulfed the platform and me. People were pushed up in wheelchairs. They came out of the wheelchairs and just kept right on walking....

The next day [we] picked up armloads of crutches and eyeglasses, and hearing aids.... It started and stopped in five minutes.

∽

Pat Robertson

"I was speaking in another language."

Marion Gordon "Pat" Robertson (1930–) was born in Lexington, Virginia, the son of A. Willis Robertson, a U.S. Senator from Virginia. Soon after his graduation from Yale Law School in 1955 he accepted Christ. He went on to earn a Master of Divinity degree from New York Biblical Seminary.

It was during his seminary years when Robertson was baptized in the Holy Spirit. He was earnestly seeking this deeper experience, but at first to no avail. His wife told him that he could meet with God just perfectly on his own at his home, and soon those words proved true. Robertson was baptized in the Holy Spirit while praying for the healing of his then-four-year-old son, Tim:

I came home from school and found Tim running a high fever.

That evening, his temperature went up to 104 degrees and by bedtime it was 105 degrees. His skin was burning hot and dry. He was unconscious and having muscle spasms. Dede, who had tried unsuccessfully to get a doctor, exclaimed, "We've got to do something! He's on the verge of convulsions!"

143

I fell on my knees. "God, do something."

Dede put Elizabeth to bed and then got on her knees with me beside Tim. I laid my hands on him and cried out again. While I was pleading with God, it flashed in my mind what a lousy father I was. How imperfect my love toward this little boy!

As these thoughts flooded my mind, I was suddenly aware of how much God loved him. I was trying to get God to do something for my son, pleading with him to love him, while all the time he loved him more than I ever could.

So, instead of begging any more, I just consciously lifted Tim up to the Lord. I gave him back to God. Suddenly I was aware of the power of God going through him. He opened his eyes and murmured, "Daddy, I gotta go to the bathroom."

He came back to his bed perspiring. I knew the healing was taking place.

"Thank you, Jesus," I began to weep. "Oh, thank you."

I gradually realized that I didn't have to ask him for anything. I could never, in a thousand lifetimes, talk him into anything he didn't want to do. And there was no need to try anyway. He loved me—and Tim—with a perfect love. That was why he healed Tim.

I felt waves of love flow over me as I began to give praise to Jesus. "Praise your holy name!" I shouted, "Praise you Jesus."

It was in this moment that I became aware my speech was garbled. I was speaking in another language. Something deep within me had been given a voice, and the Holy Spirit had supplied the words. I was aware of the sounds, but they were not of my own creation. It sounded like some African dialect, and the flow of words continued for five minutes or more.

Finally it subsided, and I was once again aware of Dede's presence in the room. She was sitting on the edge of the sofa bed, watching me. I lowered my hands and looked at her. She was wide-eyed.

"How long has this been going on?"

"What do you mean?" I answered.

"Praying in tongues."

"I just started. This was the first time."

I sat down beside her, and she reached over and gently took my hand. I felt a joining in the Spirit I hadn't felt in a long time. Softly she said, "You remember I said you didn't need to go running around all over the city seeking; I told you that God would give you the baptism right here in your own living room."

She was right.

He had.

After this experience, Robertson served with the charismatic pastor Harald Bredesen, in a Dutch Reformed congregation in Mount Vernon, New York. In 1959 he moved to Portsmouth, Virginia, where he founded the Christian Broadcasting Network (CBN) in a derelict TV station. This was the first Christian television network in the U.S. In 1978, Robertson founded CBN University, which later changed its name to Regent University. In 1986, Robertson ran for the Republican nomination for president of the United States.

∾

Mark Rutland

"It was a miracle of communication."

Mark Rutland (1947–), President of Southeastern College of the Assemblies of God, is a native Texan who was educated at the University of Maryland and the Candler School of Theology at Emory University in Atlanta. He also holds a Ph.D. from the California Graduate School of Theology. For many years Rutland was a leading speaker in the charismatic renewal of the United Methodist Church, the denomination in which he was ordained.

Dr. Rutland has distinguished himself as a preacher, pastor, writer, and missionary evangelist. In recent years he has served as a preacher at the Mount Paran Church of God in Atlanta as well as serving as senior pastor of Calvary Assembly of God Church in Winter Park, Florida. As head of the "Global Servants" ministry, he has also been involved in missionary ministries in many nations. His six books include *Launch Out Into the Deep*, the volume in which this testimony is found.

In 1977, on a mission trip to a remote village south of Tampico, Mexico, Dr. Rutland experienced one of the best-documented cases of preaching an entire sermon in a language that he did not know, Spanish. His father-in-law, who claimed to be an atheist, was present to attest to the miraculous event that night. After witnessing this miracle, he was converted. Among the many miracles that have accompanied Rutland's ministry, the following one is surely unique:

Another Mexican bus figured in one truly touching act of the Spirit. Jim and I and another group of Americans were to be in a service in a very remote mountain village southwest of Tampico. An interpreter had agreed to come out from Tampico on the bus and meet us there. The bus broke down in transit and he never arrived.

I had only a handful of Spanish words that I could string together in no more than three or four rote sentences of greeting. None of those other Americans spoke any Spanish at all except Jim Mann, whose

*modest conversational Spanish could not possibly enable him to trans-
late. He needed an interpreter himself. No one in the village, including the pastor, spoke a single word of English.*

*In a painful, stumbling conference with several Mexicans, Jim and
I agreed that the pastor should preach. I would bring a few words of
greeting in my two or three faltering sentences of Spanish. This would,
in addition to giving the villagers a gentle laugh at the American's
expense, establish a little rapport in case we ever came back.*

*As I stood and began to speak, the Spirit of the Lord did something
marvelous. Words, phrases, whole sentences tumbled out with incredible facility. I preached in Spanish for thirty-five minutes!*

*It was not like speaking in tongues exactly. I was thinking quite
clearly in English and interpreting in my mind into Spanish.
Thinking it through over the years, I have come to believe that what the
Holy Spirit was doing was to supernaturally dredge up every word of
Spanish I had heard interpreted in sermon after sermon. Perhaps those
words had taken root in my inner mind somehow to be drawn on by
the Holy Spirit in that night.*

*Whatever happened, it was a miracle of communication. In that
moment of need the Holy Spirit gifted me with Spanish that I speak
today. As it began to dawn on all in the church what was happening,
the Mexicans and the Americans began to weep in the presence of the
Lord. What a night! Seeing the power of God, many were saved and
baptized in the Holy Spirit in that place.*

William J. Seymour

"A sphere of white hot brilliance seemed to appear, draw near, and fall upon him."

Perhaps no man has been more responsible for the worldwide growth of the modern pentecostal/charismatic movement than William Joseph Seymour (1870–1922). Born in Centerville, Louisiana, to former slaves Simon and Phillis Seymour, William was given to visions of God from an early age.

In 1905, while in Houston, Texas, Seymour was introduced to Charles Fox Parham, the theological founder of the pentecostal movement. Parham, who believed that the gift of tongues was being restored to the church, invited Seymour to attend some special teachings on the subject at a school he had started. Because it was illegal in Texas for whites and blacks to sit in the same classroom, Parham allowed Seymour to listen to his classroom teachings by leaving the door ajar so he could hear from the hallway.

Parham's teachings greatly influenced Seymour, who was already a strict Holiness preacher in his own right. In January of the next year, 1906, Seymour left the city of Houston to pastor a small black Holiness Church in Los Angeles, California. After preaching that tongues was the "Bible evidence" of the baptism in the Holy Spirit, Seymour was locked out of the church.

Seymour then was invited to stay with the Richard Asberry family on Bonnie Brae Street. It was here that Pentecost first came to Los Angeles. By April, 1906, Seymour secured an old abandoned AME Church building at 312 Azusa Street in downtown Los Angeles. Here one of the greatest revivals in church history took place from 1906 to 1909 under his leadership. The Azusa Street meetings spread pentecostalism to the far reaches of the globe.

The following is an account of the night when Seymour was baptized in the Holy Spirit accompanied by speaking in tongues.

The entire company was immediately swept to its knees as by some tremendous power. At least seven—and perhaps more—lifted their voices in an awesome harmony of strange new tongues. Jennie Evans Moore, falling to her knees from the piano seat, became the first woman thus to speak.

Some rushed out to the front porch, yard, and street, shouting and speaking in tongues for all the neighborhood to hear. Little Willella Asbery ran in from the kitchen to see what was happening. Her older brother, eleven-year-old Morton, rushed in the opposite direction, frightened.

Teenager Bud Traynor stood on the front porch prophesying and preaching. Jennie Evans Moore returned to the piano and began singing in her beautiful voice what was thought to be a series of six languages with interpretations. The meeting lasted until about 10:00, everyone giving thanks for what they believed to be early Pentecost restored.

For three days they celebrated with intense joy and exuberant gladness. Crowds gathered, filling the yard and surrounding the house. Some gratefully stood near the open windows where tongues from inside could be heard.

Many white people came. The floor of the crowded wooden front porch collapsed under the strain but no one was hurt and it was soon re-braced. At times they shouted their acclaim for all to hear, at other times an awesome hush descended.

Some fell into trances for three, four, or even five hours. Unusual healings were reported. Clusters of people outside whispered reverently that God's power was falling again as in the book of Acts.

Seymour and the others believed with absolute faith this was Pentecost restored to the church as God's prophesied sign for the end of the age. Their studies had lifted their hopes to expect the Holy Spirit in a second great outpouring like the first at Jerusalem so long ago. And now to their overjoyed wonder they proclaimed that God had done it again in their midst at 214 North Bonnie Brae Street on April 9th, 1906, in Los Angeles, California, USA. Suddenly they became a movement joined by many who shared these views.

On the third night of the spiritual explosion, April 12th, Maundy Thursday, Seymour received his personal Pentecost. The night was late and about to slip away. Most of the company were too tired to continue praying. Two of them remained on their knees together in prayer, determined to "pray through." One was Seymour, the other a white man.

Finally, the white friend faltered, exhausted. "It is not the time," he said wearily. "Yes it is," replied Seymour, "I am not going to give up." He kept on, alone, and in response to his last prayer, a sphere of white hot brilliance seemed to appear, draw near, and fall upon him.

Divine love melted his heart; he sank to the floor seemingly unconscious. Words of deep healing and encouragement spoke to him. As from a great distance he heard unutterable words being uttered—was it angelic adoration and praise? Slowly he realized the indescribably lovely language belonged to him, pouring from his innermost being. A broad smile wreathed his face. At last, he arose and happily embraced those around him.

Demos Shakarian

"That which you see now will soon come to pass."

Demos Shakarian (1913–93) was born in Downey, California. His parents had fled their native Armenia after a prophet warned them of a coming disaster to fall upon the land. By leaving, they later escaped the Armenian holocaust.

In Armenia, the Shakarians had belonged to a religious movement that had similarities to modern pentecostalism. After settling in Los Angeles, Demos' father attended the Azusa Street revival, after which they organized an Armenian pentecostal congregation. Demos was saved at an early age and was baptized in the Spirit in 1926.

In time, he became a very successful businessman. By the 1950s he owned one of the largest private dairies in the world. Later in life he felt that God wanted him to start a ministry to reach out to other businessmen. Although he was not a preacher, Shakarian organized many evangelistic crusades for such evangelists as Charles Price and Oral Roberts.

In 1951, after an Oral Roberts Crusade in Los Angeles, Shakarian organized the Full Gospel Business Men's Fellowship International (FGBMFI). By the end of the first year he became extremely discouraged by the slow growth of the organization. At his lowest point of frustration, he received a vision that in time became the central inspiration of the

FGBMFI. The following is his account of what happened on that fateful night in Downey, California.

Just as he was about to give up in despair, Shakarian experienced a transforming vision which infused him with an inspiration and zeal that re-ignited his dreams. On Friday night December 26, 1952, the Shakarians had in their home a house guest, Tommy Hicks, a little-known pentecostal evangelist. That night, Shakarian confided to Hicks that since so little interest had been shown to his idea, the next day would be the last meeting in Clifton's Cafeteria.

Late that evening, Shakarian suggested that everyone else in the house go to bed while he went into the living room to pray "till he heard from God, no matter how long it took." His place of prayer was the red Oriental rug that covered the living room floor. As he began to pray it seemed that "the heavens were made of brass." Then he experienced a vision that forever changed his life and that of the infant FGBMFI organization.

As the vision continued, his wife, Rose, came into the room and began playing the organ softly. The experience that followed not only changed the course of his life, but the future course of Full Gospel Business Men's Fellowship.

In an apparent ecstasy lasting for several hours, Shakarian was taken around the world in a vision where he was able to see all the continents from the air. As he looked down, he could see, as through a telephoto lens, men as frozen statues, cold and lifeless. In Africa, Latin America, Europe, and Asia, he saw the same scene, "brown faces, black faces, white faces—everyone rigid, wretched, each locked in its own private death."

Then he made another circuit of the globe and this time millions of people had come to life. "This time heads were raised, eyes shone with joy. Hands were lifted towards heaven ... everywhere death had turned to life."

At this point, Rose, while playing the organ, began to prophesy words of encouragement, saying: "You are in the will of the Lord and it was for this reason that you were born." Then she spoke in tongues and again prophesied, saying, "That which you see now will soon come to pass." Meanwhile, Tommy Hicks, who was in the guest bedroom, was receiving a similar vision for a great revival in Argentina.

∾

A. B. Simpson

"A mighty baptism of the Holy Ghost in his complete pentecostal fullness."

Albert Benjamin Simpson (1843–1919) was born on Prince Edward Island, Canada, in 1843. Early in life he had felt God's call to ministry, and in 1865 he became pastor of Knox Presbyterian Church in Ontario. He later accepted a call to the Chestnut Street Presbyterian Church in Louisville, Kentucky.

While there, a revival broke out in the church, and Simpson had a definite deeper experience with God which he termed "the fullness of blessing of Christ." This began a deeper seeking for even more of God's power and presence in his life.

Plagued by constant ill health and sickness from his youth, he began, soon after 1881, to get worse. The doctors told him he had only a few months to live. However, God granted him a total healing from all his former sicknesses, and he went on to have many more fruitful years of service for God.

In those later years he wrote more than seventy books on the Bible, composed numerous hymns, started a Bible and missionary training school, and organized two societies, the Christian Alliance in 1887 and the International Missionary Alliance in 1889. Those two societies came together in 1897 to form the Christian and Missionary Alliance that we know today.

Simpson was never just satisfied with the baptism of the Holy Spirit as he had been taught in the higher life movement. He wanted more and more of God's presence and was constantly asking God for fresh impartation. In 1907, a mighty wave of pentecostal revival swept the Nyack Bible School campus with many manifestations of tongues and prophecies. At this point the CMA was on the brink of joining the mainstream of the pentecostal movement.

Although he never fully accepted the pentecostal teaching on tongues as "initial evidence," Simpson took a middle ground approach that was later summarized as "seek not, forbid not." Yet, to the end, his diary showed that he was an earnest seeker for a baptism in the Holy Spirit experience with the possibility of speaking in tongues. In the end, he seems to have been disappointed that he failed to speak in tongues. Here are some of his journal entries for 1907 that demonstrate his desire to experience more of God.

July 28

On the closing Saturday of the Nyack Convention I received, as I waited in the after meeting, a distinct touch of the mighty power of the Holy Spirit—a kind of breaking through, accompanied by a sense of awe and a lighting up of my senses. It was as if a wedge of light and power were being driven through my inmost being and I all broken up [sic].

154

I welcomed it and felt disappointed when the meeting was abruptly closed by the leader, for I was conscious of a peculiar power resting upon us all and continuing to fill me. I carried it home with me, and for several days the deep sense remained as a sort of "weight of love," in addition to the ordinary and quiet sense of God I have felt so long.

August 9

On this Friday afternoon I retired, as I have done for so many years, to the place in the woods where God healed me in August 1881 and renewed my covenant of healing again as I have done every year since.

At the same time I pressed upon him a new claim for a mighty baptism of the Holy Ghost in his complete pentecostal fullness, embracing all the gifts and graces of the Spirit for my special need at this time and for the new conditions and needs of my life and work. He met me as I lay upon my face before him with a distinct illumination, and then as the Presence began to fade and I cried out to him to stay, he bade me believe and take it all by simple faith as I had taken my healing twenty-six years before. I did so, and was enabled definitely to believe and claim it all and rest in him.

Then he gave me distinctly Isaiah 49:8, "In an acceptable time have I heard thee, etc." Also Acts 1:5, "Ye shall be baptized with the Holy Ghost not many days hence." I knew that I had been baptized with the Holy Ghost before but I was made to understand that God had a deeper and fuller baptism for me and all that day and evening I was as sure of the coming of his Spirit to me in great power as if I had already received the most wonderful manifestation of his presence.

I was accustomed at Old Orchard to spend hours every night waiting upon him and praying about the meetings, and he often rested upon me in mighty realization and wondrously guided and blessed the work, but I felt there was MORE.

Barton Stone

"The singing exercise is more unaccountable than anything else I ever saw."

The America Camp Meeting was born on the Kentucky frontier in 1801 at a place called Cane Ridge. Starting as a "sacramental" (communion) service in the Cane Ridge Presbyterian Church, the worshippers soon experienced many spiritual manifestations that beggared the imagination. Some of these included running, the "holy dance," the "holy laugh," and being "slain in the Spirit." Although the worshippers at Cane Ridge were Presbyterians, Baptists, and Methodists, their Cane Ridge meeting was later described by historians as "America's Pentecost." As many as 25,000 persons are said to have come to attend these services that many critics charged were out of control.

After 1801, the camp meeting became a staple of American religious life, especially among the Methodists. Also issuing from Cane Ridge was a new family of "Restorationist" denominations known today as the Churches of Christ and the Disciples of Christ. The two best-known leaders in these new churches were Alexander Campbell and Barton Stone (1772–1844).

In 1847 Stone's autobiography was published. In it, he described his own eyewitness accounts of what he called the bodily "exercises" at Cane Ridge. Although he was greatly criticized for defending these manifestations, he insisted until his death that they were genuine works of the Holy Spirit. Many modern-day pentecostals believe that the "singing exercises" were a type of singing in tongues.

Here's a condensed account of these various ecstatic manifestations:

Falling

The falling exercise was very common among all classes, the saints and sinners of every age and every grade, from the philosopher to the clown. The subject of this exercise would, generally, with a piercing scream, fall like a log on the floor, earth, or mud, and appear as dead.

At a meeting, two gay young ladies, sisters, both fell, with a shriek of distress, and lay for more than an hour apparently in a lifeless state. At length they began to exhibit symptoms of life, by crying fervently for mercy, and then relapsed into the same death-like state, with an awful gloom on their countenances. After a while, the gloom on the face of one was succeeded by a heavenly smile, and she cried out, "Precious Jesus!" and rose up and spoke of the love of God.

The Jerks

Sometimes the subject of the jerks would be affected in some one member of the body, and sometimes in the whole system. When the head alone was affected, it would be jerked backward and forward, or from side to side, so quickly that the features of the face could not be distinguished. When the whole system was affected, I have seen the person stand in one place, and jerk backward and forward in quick succession, their head nearly touching the floor behind and before.

Dancing

The dancing exercise generally began with the jerks, then the jerks would cease. The smile of heaven shone on the countenance of the subject, and assimilated to angels appeared the whole person. Sometimes the motion was quick and sometimes slow. Thus they continued to move forward and backward in the same track or alley till nature seemed exhausted, and they would fall prostrate on the floor or earth.

Barking
The barking exercise (as opposers contemptuously called it) was nothing but the jerks. A person affected with the jerks would often make a grunt, or bark, if you please, from the suddenness of the jerk.

Laughing
It was a loud, hearty laughter, but one [that] excited laughter in none else. The subject appeared rapturously solemn, and his laughter excited solemnity in saints and sinners. It is truly indescribable.

Running
The running exercise was nothing more than that persons [who,] feeling something of these bodily agitations, through fear, attempted to run away and thus escape from them. But it commonly happened that they ran not far before they fell or became so greatly agitated that they could proceed no farther.

Singing
The singing exercise is more unaccountable than anything else I ever saw. The subject in a very happy state of mind would sing most melodiously, not from the mouth or nose, but entirely in the breast, the sounds issuing thence. Such music silenced everything, and attracted the attention of all. It was most heavenly. None could ever be tired of hearing it.

༐

A.J. Tomlinson

"As I went down I yielded myself up to God."

Ambrose Jessup Tomlinson (1865–1943) was born near Westfield, Indiana, into a Quaker family, but his parents were only nominally involved in church or spiritual things. At age twenty-four he made a personal decision for Christ. He then became involved with the Holiness movement and claimed to be sanctified. By 1901 he had attended God's Bible School in Cincinnati, joined Frank Sandford's "Church of the Living God" in Shiloh, Maine, and begun a ministry as a "colporteur" (salesman) for the American Bible Society in the mountains of western North Carolina.

While in North Carolina, Tomlinson came across the Holiness Church at Camp Creek, which had been organized in 1902. He joined in 1903 and was immediately made pastor of the church with the understanding that this was the "Church of God of the Bible." From this base, he became the organizing genius of what became the Church of God with headquarters in Cleveland, Tennessee.

In January of 1907, Tomlinson traveled to Memphis, Tennessee, to learn more about the pentecostal movement that was spreading rapidly from Azusa Street. He then invited G.B. Cashwell, a member of the Pentecostal Holiness Church of North Carolina who had spoken in tongues at Azusa Street, to speak in the 1908 General Assembly of the church.

While Cashwell was speaking, Tomlinson experienced one of the most vivid pentecostal baptisms recorded in all the literature of the movement. The following account is his testimony of his experience, which guaranteed that the Church of God would become one of the leading pentecostal denominations in the United States. It is contained in his personal diary from 1899 to 1943, which he titled "A Journal of Happenings."

Our assembly consumed the last three days of last week. Saturday night Bro. Cashwell preached and on Sunday, yesterday, at nearly the close of his discourse, the Spirit so affected me that I slid down off my chair onto the floor, or on the rostrum, and as I went down I yielded myself up to God; and after a considerable of agony and groans my jaws seemed to be set, my lips were moved and twisted about as if an examination of them were being made.

After that my tongue was operated on in like manner, also my eyes. Several examinations seemed to be taken, and every limb of my body was operated on in like manner, and finally, while lying on my back both of my feet were raised right up in the air several times. Then I felt myself lifted as in a great sheet of power of some kind, and moved in the air in the direction my feet pointed.

As I lay there great joy flooded my soul, my hands clapped together, and I glorified God without any effort on my part. At other times the most excruciating pain and agony, but my spirit said yes to God at every point. My mind was finally carried to Central America, and I was shown the awful condition of the people there. After a paroxysm of suffering the Holy Ghost spoke through my lips and tongue beyond my control, and which seemed to be the very language of the Indian tribes there.

Then after a little rest I was carried in mind to all of South America, and of all the black pictures that was surely the blackest. Then my mind settled on Brazil. Then, after another paroxysm of suffering, the Spirit spoke again in another tongue.

After a little relaxation I was shown Chile, with the same effects and results. In like manner Patagonia, down among those illiterate Indians. At each place I was shown I gave assent to go to them. From Patagonia to Africa, and on to Jerusalem, and while here awful suffering in my body. I never can describe it.

After every paroxysm of suffering came a tongue. From there away up to Northern Russia, then to France, then to Japan. Then I seemed to get back to the U.S., but soon I was taken up north among the Eskimaux. While here the language seemed to be a little like the bark of a dog. Then somewhere in Canada.

Then I came back to Cleveland, and I seemed to be asked if I was willing to testify or speak on the public square of the city. Without any effort my spirit seemed to give consent. Then to Chattanooga. From there my mind seemed to be carried along the railroad to Cincinnati and right on through the city to my old home in Indiana.

∾

John Wesley

"The power of God came mightily upon us."

Born in Lincolnshire, England, John Wesley (1703–91) was the fifteenth child in a family of nineteen children. He was a fourth-generation clergyman in the Church of England. John was an extremely bright child and started seminary training at Oxford University at age seventeen. In addition to his native English he was fluent in Latin, Greek, Hebrew, French, and German.

Although Wesley thought his relationship with God had been secured from his youth, he had an encounter with some Moravian missionaries that greatly impressed him on an overseas trip to the American colonies. Upon his return to England he soon had a personal conversion experience in which he knew he trusted Christ alone for salvation.

Yet Wesley hungered and thirsted for more of God. He wanted to be filled with God in order to carry out the purpose he felt God had for his life. His evangelical conversion took place on May 24, 1738, in London. He said of this experience:

I felt my heart strangely warmed. I felt I did trust in Christ alone, for salvation; and an assurance was given me, that he had taken away my sins, and even mine, and saved me from the law of sin and death.

This powerful encounter with God would forever change Wesley, and it seemed to empower him for unbelievable acts of service that would last well into his late eighties. Wesley rose regularly at 4:00 A.M. for communion with God and then spent the rest of the day traveling from city to city, preaching from dawn to dusk. He started the reform movement known as "Methodism" within the Church of England. In every town he ministered he organized "classes," which were the forerunner to modern small groups (or "cell" groups) for mutual ministry. He felt that people needed the fellowship, accountability, and study time that the groups afforded.

Wesley was a prolific writer and master organizer, and his

partner and brother, Charles, composed thousands of Christian hymns for the new movement. By the time of his death at age eighty-seven, one third of England belonged to the Methodist movement. He had started more than 12,000 of his cell groups across the nation, traveled more than 225,000 miles by horseback, preached more than 40,000 sermons, and saw tens of thousands of people receive Christ as Lord.

Since Wesley taught a "second blessing" of entire sanctification, many people have conjectured about when and how he might have received the experience. Many Methodists and Holiness people point to the meeting that Wesley had with the great revivalist George Whitefield, along with some other prominent Methodists at a union meeting of the Methodist Societies at Fetter Lane. Here, they say, Wesley was "sanctified" through the Holy Spirit. Here is his description of that event:

Monday, January 1, 1739
Mr. Hall, Kinchin, Ingham, Whitefield, Hutchins, and my brother Charles were present at our love feast in Fetter Lane, with about sixty of our brethren. About three in the morning, as we were continuing instant in prayer, the power of God came mightily upon us, insomuch that many cried out for exceeding joy, and many fell to the ground. As soon as we recovered a little from the awe and amazement at the presence of his majesty, we broke out with one voice, "We praise thee, O God, we acknowledge thee to be the Lord."

❧

Smith Wigglesworth

"At last, I had received the real baptism in the Holy Spirit."

The great English healing evangelist Smith Wigglesworth (1859–1947) was unknown outside of his hometown until age forty-eight, when he received the baptism of the Spirit. Wigglesworth was never afforded the opportunity to get an education because he had to begin working at age six to help support his poor family. Consequently, he could barely read or write until late in his adult life.

His wife, Polly, a preacher and mission worker, taught him to read using the Bible. A strong faith in God's Word and truth later convinced Smith that he should never read anything again but the Word of God. Newspapers were not allowed in his home.

In 1907, Wigglesworth heard about the pentecostal baptism in the Holy Spirit that was being poured out in an Anglican Church in Sunderland, England, under the pastoral direction of the Vicar, Alexander Boddy. He later recalled the ensuing events.

Pastor Boddy, who was vicar of the Episcopal (Anglican) Church where those first pentecostal meetings were held, gave out a notice that there would be a waiting meeting all night on Tuesday. It was a very precious time and the presence of the Lord was very wonderful, but I did not hear anyone speak in tongues. At 2:30 in the morning, Brother Boddy said, "we better close the meeting." I was disappointed, for I would have liked to stay there all night....

For four days I wanted nothing but God. But after that, I felt I should leave for home, and I went to the Episcopal vicarage to say goodbye. I said to Mrs. Boddy, the vicar's wife: "I am going away, but I have not received the tongues yet."

She answered, "It is not tongues you need, but the baptism."

"I have received the baptism, Sister," I protested, "but I would like to have you lay hands on me before I leave." She laid her hands on and then had to go out of the room.

The fire fell. It was a wonderful time as I was there with God alone. He bathed me in power.

I was conscious of the cleansing of the precious blood, and I cried out, "Clean! Clean! Clean!" I was filled with the joy of the consciousness of the cleansing. I was given a vision in which I saw the Lord Jesus Christ. I beheld the empty cross, and I saw him exalted at the right hand of God the Father.

I could speak no longer in English but I began to praise him in other tongues as the Spirit of God gave me utterance. I knew then, although I might have received anointings previously, that now, at last, I had received the real baptism in the Holy Spirit as they received on the day of Pentecost.

After being healed of a ruptured appendix, Smith gained faith to pray for others with similar conditions. Eventually he began praying for other conditions as well, and soon people were being healed of every infirmity and disease imaginable when he prayed and laid hands upon them. Wigglesworth had a true compassion for the sick, weeping many times over the letters he received asking him to come and pray for the sick in some community. Several publicized cases of the dead being raised occurred in his ministry as well.

Ironically, he later developed very painful kidney stones, and he was never healed of them. Many times in intense pain he would preach and minister healing to others while he himself never complained about his own condition.

The following is Wigglesworth's account of a healing service in Sweden in 1920.

It was a time of visitation from on high. I dare to say that hundreds of people received Jesus as their Savior, thousands were healed of all kinds of diseases, also thousands of people awoke to a new life, and many received the baptism of the Holy Spirit as on the day of Pentecost. For all this we give the glory to Jesus. Here are a few examples of miracles my eyes have seen....

It was wonderful to notice, as the ministry continued, the effect upon the people as the power of the Lord came over them. Some lifted their hands crying, "I am healed!" Some fell on the platform, overpowered by the power of the Spirit, and had to be helped down. A young blind girl, as she was ministered to, cried out, "Oh, how many windows there are in this hall!"

During the three weeks the meetings continued, the great chapel was crowded daily, multitudes being healed and many saved. The testimony meetings were wonderful. One said, "I was deaf; they prayed, and Jesus healed me." Another: "I had consumption, and I am free." And so on.

❧

J. Rodman Williams

"Then I knew it was happening: I was being filled with his Holy Spirit."

John Rodman Williams (1918–) is known as the major systematic theologian produced by the charismatic movement. Born to Presbyterian parents in North Carolina, Williams earned a Ph.D. in the Philosophy of Religion from Columbia University and Union Theological Seminary in New York City in 1954. After serving several pastorates, he became professor of systematic theology at Austin Presbyterian Seminary, where he served from 1959 to 1972.

In 1965 Rodman's life was drastically changed when he experienced baptism in the Holy Spirit while alone in his study. He then worked with David du Plessis in spreading charismatic renewal throughout Europe and the United States. After this, he served as president of Melodyland School of Theology in Anaheim, California, and as professor of systematic theology at Regent University in Virginia Beach, Virginia. His major work is *Renewal Theology*, which was published in three volumes from 1988 to 1992.

The following testimony is his account of his baptism in the Holy Spirit.

Then came Wednesday, the day before Thanksgiving—THE DAY!
I felt at ease, and began to turn to letters on my desk. One letter was

from a pastor who described his experience of recently visiting the seminary and being prayed for by a student to receive the gift of the Holy Spirit. He wrote about how later he began to speak in tongues and praise God mightily.

As I read and re-read the letter, the words somehow seemed to leap off the page, and I found myself being overcome. I was soon on my knees practically in tears praying for the Holy Spirit, and pounding the chair—asking, seeking, knocking—in a way I never had done before. Now I intensely yearned for the gift of the Holy Spirit.

Then I stood and began to beseech God to break me open, to fill me to the fullest—with sometimes an almost torturous cry to what was in myself to possess my total being. But for a time all seemed to no avail. With hands outstretched I then began to pray to God the Father, Son, and Holy Spirit—and mixed in with the entreaty was a verse of Scripture I kept crying out: "Bless the Lord, O my soul; and all that is within me, bless his holy name!"

I yearned to bless the Lord with all my being—my total self, body, soul, and spirit—all that was within me. Then I knew it was happening: I was being filled with his Holy Spirit.

Also, for the first time I earnestly desired to speak in tongues because the English language seemed totally incapable of expressing the inexpressible glory and love of God. Instead of articulating rational words, I began to ejaculate sounds of any kind, praying that somehow the Lord would use them. Suddenly I realized that something drastic was happening: My noises were being left behind, and I was off with such utterance, such words as I had never heard before.

Waves after wave, torrent after torrent, poured out. It was utterly fantastic. I was doing it and yet I was not.

I seemed to be utterly detached and utterly involved. To some degree I could control the speed of the words—but not much; they were pouring

168

out at a terrific rate. I could stop the flow whenever I wanted, but in operation I had absolutely no control over the nature or articulation of the sounds.

My tongue, my jaws, my vocal cords were totally possessed—but not by me. Tears began to stream down my face—joy unutterable, amazement incredible. Over and over I felt borne down to the floor by the sheer weight of it all, and sometimes I would cry: "I don't believe it; I don't believe it!" It was so completely unlike anything I had ever known before.

Finally, I sat down in my chair, but still felt buoyed up as if by a vast inner power. I knew I was on earth, but it was as if heaven had intersected it—and I was in both. God was so much there that I scarcely moved a muscle: his delicate, lush, ineffable presence.

Suddenly, it dawned on me that I had not yet so much as glanced at a Bible. Quickly I opened one up to Acts 2. To be sure, I had read the pentecostal story many times, but this was incredibly different. I felt I was there.

As I read the words with my eyes and my mind, and began to do so out loud, I knew I could speak, as I read, in a tongue. This I did, verse after verse—reading the account of the filling with the Holy Spirit, speaking in other tongues, and what immediately followed—reading all this with the accompaniment of my own new tongue! By the time I arrived at the verse, "Being therefore exalted at the right hand of God, and having received from the Father the promise of the Holy Spirit, he [Christ] has poured out this which you see and hear" (see Acts 2:33), I was so overwhelmed that I could only stand and sing, "Praise God, praise God," over and over again.

The whole event lasted about an hour. Then I felt strangely impelled by the Holy Spirit to move around the house, room after room, each time to speak out with a prayer in the tongue. I was not sure why I was *doing this, but it was as if the Holy Spirit was blessing each spot, each corner. Truly, as it later turned out, he was preparing a sanctuary for his presence and action.*

❧

Maria Woodworth-Etter

"The power of the Holy Ghost came down as a cloud."

One of the early female pentecostal pioneers was Maria Woodworth-Etter (1844–1924), born in New Lisbon, Ohio. Neither of her parents were Christians, and her father had a problem with alcohol. As a child she received no religious instruction, although her little heart was always tender towards the things of God. Maria was converted at age thirteen when a minister took an interest in her and prayed for her. He prayed that she would be a shining light to all the world.

Maria never questioned God's plan or goodness, even though eventually four of her children died from sickness before the age of seven. Ironically, God would later place a healing mantle upon his servant Maria, and she would be used to heal all manner of sickness in others.

Beginning as an evangelist in the Holiness movement, after 1906 Woodworth-Etter became the most powerful healing evangelist in the pentecostal movement. The record of healings in her long ministry are unmatched in all the literature of pentecostal signs and wonders.

Although God used Maria many times to heal others, he also used her to announce judgment prophetically on sinners as well. In 1883 in Monroeville, Indiana, she was invited to minister in a church that was known to be very dry. Maria tells what happened one night during the meetings.

One night I was pleading with sinners to accept the invitation to be present at the marriage supper of God's only-begotten Son. I felt death was very near. I told them someone was refusing for the last time; the coffin and winding-sheet were near.

Oh, how I pleaded with them to accept while there was mercy. One old man was so convicted that he could not stand it. He would not yield. He left the house, cursing the Methodist church. He thought to run away from God.

But swift judgment was on his track. In going out of town a train ran over him and killed him. The next morning before 7 o'clock they told me he was in his winding sheet and ready for the coffin.

Here is Maria's account of receiving the baptism in the Holy Spirit.

I want the reader to understand that at this time I had a good experience, a pure heart, was full of the love of God, but was not qualified for God's work. I knew that I was but a worm. God would have to take a worm to thresh a mountain.

Then I asked God to give me the power he gave the Galilean fishermen—to anoint me for service. I came like a child asking for bread. I looked for it.

God did not disappoint me. The power of the Holy Ghost came down as a cloud. It was brighter than the sun. I was covered and wrapped up in it. My body was light as the air.

It seemed that heaven came down. I was baptized with the Holy Ghost, and fire, and power which has never left me. Oh, praise the

Lord! There was liquid fire, and the angels were all around in the fire and glory. It is through the Lord Jesus Christ and by his power that I have stood before hundreds of thousands of men and women, proclaiming the unsearchable riches of Christ.

Many churches in her day did not ordain women, so many people criticized Woodworth-Etter for preaching. Yet she never questioned her call to ministry. She defended her right to minister this way:

As I continued to read my Bible I saw that in all ages of the world the Lord raised up of his own choosing, men, women, and children—Miriam, Deborah, Hannah, Hulda, Anna, Phoebe, Narcissus, Tryphena, Persis, Julia, and the Marys, and the sisters who were coworkers with Paul in the gospel, whose names were in the Book of Life, and many other women whose labors are mentioned with praise. Even the children were made the instruments of his praise and glory.

The more I investigated the more I found to condemn me. There was the Master giving one, two, and five talents, and the moral obligation of each person receiving them and their several rewards. I had one talent, which was hidden away.

By the prophet Joel we learn that one special feature of the gospel dispensation shall be "Your sons and your daughters shall prophesy, your old men shall dream dreams, your young men shall see visions: And also upon the servants and upon the handmaids in those days will I pour out my spirit (Jl 2:28-29). It seems by the prophet Joel, that the last days were to be particularly conspicuous for this kind of prophesying. We cannot reverse God's decree for Jesus said, "Heaven and earth shall pass away: but my words shall not pass away" (Mk 13:31).

Sources

Augustine, St.

Eddie Ensley, *Sounds of Wonder: Speaking in Tongues in the Catholic Tradition* (New York: Paulist, 1977), 19-20. Copyright 1977 by the Missionary Society of St. Paul the Apostle in the State of New York, N.J. Used with permission of Paulist Press. www.paulistpress.com

Barratt, Thomas Ball

Thomas Ball Barratt, *When the Fire Fell: And an Outline of My Life* (Oslo, Norway: Alfons Houser & Soner, 1927), 129-30. Reprinted by the Garland Publishing Company in the Higher Life Series. N.Y., 1985.

Bartleman, Frank

Frank Bartleman, *How "Pentecost" Came to Los Angeles* (Los Angeles: Self-published, 1925), 167-73.

Bennett, Dennis

Dennis Bennett, *Nine O'Clock in the Morning* (Plainfield, N.J.: Bridge, 1970), 15-21.

Bonnke, Reinhard

Reinhard Bonnke, *The Millennium Crusade Videotape* (Lagos, Nigeria: Christ for All Nations, 2001). Used by permission of Reinhard Bonnke.

Branham, William

Owen Jorgenson, *Supernatural: The Life of William Branham, Book Four* (Tucson, Ariz.: Tucson Tabernacle, 2001), 30-33.

Bredesen, Harald

Harald Bredesen, *Yes, Lord* (Tulsa, Okla.: Praise, 1982), 58-59.

Buckalew, J.W.

Charles Conn, *The Evangel Reader* (Cleveland, Tenn.: Pathway, 1958), 152-53. Used by permission of Pathway Press.

Carter, Howard

Colin Whittaker, *Seven Pentecostal Pioneers* (Springfield, Mo.: Gospel, 1983), 104-7.

Cashwell, G.B.

G. B. Cashwell, "Came 3000 Miles for His Pentecost," *The Apostolic Faith*, December 1906, 3.

Chambers, Oswald

Martin Wells Knapp, *God's Revivalist,* January 17, 1907. Quoted in Kevin Moser and Larry Smith, eds., *God's Clock Keeps Perfect Time: God's Bible School: The First 100 Years* (Cincinnati, Ohio: Revivalist, 2000), 47.

Crawford, Florence

Larry Martin, *The True Believers: Part Two* (Joplin, Mo.: Christian Life, 1999), 137-42. Used by permission of Christian Life Books.

Derstine, Gerald

Gerald Derstine, *Following the Fire* (Plainfield, N.J.: Bridge, 1980), 116-17.

Dowie, John Alexander

Gordon Lindsay, *The Life of John Alexander Dowie* (Dallas: The Voice of Healing, 1951), 140-43. Used by permission of Christ for the Nations.

du Plessis, David

Bob Slosser, *A Man Called Mr. Pentecost, As Told to Bob Slosser* (Plainfield, N.J.: Logos International, 1977), 34-35.

Durham, William H.

William Durham, "A Chicago Evangelist's Pentecost," *Apostolic Faith*, February-March 1907, 4.

Finney, Charles

Charles G. Finney, *An Autobiography* (Old Tappan, N.J.: F.H.
    Revell, 1908), 20; Charles G. Finney, *God's Provision of
    Power* (Clinton, N.Y.: Williams, 2002), 179-80.

Flower, Alice Reynolds

Wayne Warner, *Touched by the Fire* (Plainfield, N.J.: Logos
    International, 1978), 33-35; Ralph Harris, *Spoken by the
    Spirit* (Springfield, Mo.: Gospel, 1973), 69-70. Used by
    permission of Wayne Warner.

Francis of Assisi, St.

Ensley, 58-61.

Graham, Billy

Thomas Zimmerman, Assemblies of God Board of Missions
    Minutes, December 17, 1982; Ken Kaunley, taped inter-
    view with the author, May 2002; Pastor D.W. Wartenbee,
    taped testimony, Bethel Assembly of God in Spring-
    field, Missouri, May 2002. Testimony tapes used by
    permission of D.W. Wartenbee and Sam Kaunley.

Guerra, Elena

Elena Guerra, *Rebirth in the Holy Spirit* (Rome: Giuliano
    Agresti, 1985), 22-35. See also Kim Kollins, *Burning
    Bush: A Return to the Upper Room in Adoration and
    Intercession* (Kelheim, Germany: Self-published, rev. ed.,
    2001), 135-36.

Guyon, Madame Jeanne

James Gilchrist Lawson, *Deeper Experiences of Famous Christians*
    (Anderson, Indiana: Warner Press, 1911), 74-75.

Hagin, Kenneth

Kenneth Hagin, "From the Archives," *Word of Faith,* February
    2002, 18.

Hayford, Jack

Jack Hayford, *The Beauty of Spiritual Language: A Journey Toward the Heart of God* (Dallas: Word, 1992), 77-80. Used by permission of Jack Hayford.

Haywood, G. T.

Paul D. Dugas, *The Life and Writings of Elder G.T. Haywood* (Portland, Ore.: Apostolic, 1968), 9-10.

Holmes, Nickles J.

Nickles J. Holmes, *Life Sketches and Sermons* (Franklin Springs, Ga.: Pentecostal Holiness Church, 1909), 144-47.

Hoover, Willis C.

Dean Helland and Alice Rasmussen, *La Iglesia Metodista Pentecostal: Ayer Y Hoy* (Santiago, Chile: Plan Mundial, 1987), 56-57. Used by permission of Dean Helland.

Irving, Edward

Gordon Strachan, *The Pentecostal Theology of Edward Irving* (London: Dartman, Longman and Todd, 1973), 99-115.

Irwin, Benjamin Hardin

B. H. Irwin, "My Pentecostal Baptism—A Christmas Gift," *Triumphs of Faith*, May 1906, 114-17.

Jeffreys, Stephen

Colin Whittaker, *Seven Pentecostal Pioneers* (Springfield, Mo.: Gospel, 1983), 45-61.

John Paul II, Pope

Oreste Pesare, ed., *"Then Peter Stood Up ...": Collection of the Popes' Addresses to the Catholic Charismatic Renewal from Its Origins to the Year 2000* (Rome: ICCRS, 2000), 76-77.

King, Joseph H.

Joseph H. King and Blanche L. King, *Yet Speaketh: Memoirs of the Late Bishop Joseph H. King* (Franklin Springs, Ga.: Pentecostal Holiness Church, 1949), 37-39, 120-21. Used by permission of LifeSprings Resources.

Kuhlman, Kathryn

Jamie Buckingham, *Daughter of Destiny: Kathryn Kuhlman ... Her Story* (Plainfield, N.J.: Logos, 1976), 106-9.

McCarthy, Joan

Ralph Harris, *Spoken by the Spirit* (Springfield, Mo.: Gospel, 1973), 63-65; quoted from *New Covenant,* January 1973, 20-28.

MacNutt, Francis

Francis MacNutt, *Overcome by the Spirit* (Grand Rapids, Mich.: Chosen, 1990), 18-20.

McPherson, Aimee Semple

Raymond Cox, *The Foursquare Gospel* (Los Angeles: The Foursquare Gospel, 1969), 4-6.

Mahan, Asa

Asa Mahan, *Baptism of the Holy Spirit* (1870; reprint, Clinton, N.Y.: Williams, 2002), vi-vii.

Mansfield, Patti Gallagher

Kevin and Dorothy Ranaghan, *Catholic Pentecostals* (New York: Paulist, 1969), 34-35.

Moody, Dwight L.

James Gilchrist Lawson, *Deeper Experiences of Famous Christians* (Anderson, Ind.: Warner, 1911), 240-49.

Moore, Jennie

Jennie Moore, "Music From Heaven," *The Apostolic Faith,* May 1907, 3.

Muse, Dan T.

Harold Paul, *From Printer's Devil to Bishop* (Franklin Springs, Ga.: Advocate Press, 1976), 9-24. Used by permission of LifeSprings Resources.

Myland, David Wesley

David Wesley Myland, *The Latter Rain Covenant* (Chicago: Evangel, 1910), 213-14.

Ozman, Agnes

Agnes Ozman La Berge, *What God Hath Wrought: The Life and Work of Mrs. Agnes N.O. La Berge, Nee Miss Agnes N. Ozman* (Chicago: Herald, 1921), 28-29.

Parham, Charles

Sarah E. Parham, *The Life of Charles F. Parham, Founder of the Apostolic Faith Movement* (Joplin, Mo.: Joplin Printing, 1944), 52-53.

Paul, Jonathan

Ernst Geist, *Jonathan Paul: Ein Knecht Jesu Christi, Leben und Werk 2* (Altdorf Germany: Missionbuch Handlung und Verlag, 1965), 25-34.

Paul VI, Pope

Pesare, 17-25.

Pethrus, Lewi

Lewi Pethrus, *A Spiritual Memoir* (Plainfield, N.J.: Logos International, 1973), 22-25.

Ramabai, Pandita

Nicol MacNicol and Vishal Mangalwadi, *What Liberates a Woman? The Story of Pandita Ramabai* (New Delhi: Nivedit Good, 1996), 109-71.

Ranaghan, Kevin

Kevin and Dorothy Ranaghan, *Catholic Pentecostals* (New York: Paulist, 1969), 42-43; Vinson Synan, *In the Latter Days: The Outpouring of the Holy Spirit in the Twentieth Century,* (reprint, Fairfax, Va.: Xulon, 2001), 111-12.

Roberts, Oral

Oral Roberts, "Letter," *The Pentecostal Holiness Advocate,* July 11, 1935, 14. Quoted in David Edwin Harrell, *Oral Roberts: An American Life* (Indianapolis, Ind.: Indiana University Press, 1985), 106.

Robertson, Pat

Pat Robertson, *Shout It From the Housetops: Pat Robertson With Jamie Buckingham* (Plainfield, N.J.: Logos International, 1972), 62-68.

Rutland, Mark

Mark Rutland, *Launch Out Into the Deep* (Lakeland, Fla.: Global Servants, 1987), 59-60.

Seymour, William J.

Douglas J. Nelson, "For Such a Time as This: The Story of Bishop William J. Seymour and the Azusa Street Revival," Unpublished Ph.D. dissertation, University of Birmingham, UK, 1981, 191-92. Used by permission.

Shakarian, Demos

John Sherrill, *The Happiest People on Earth: The Long Awaited Personal Story of Demos Shakarian as told to John and Elizabeth Sherrill* (Old Tappan, N.J.: Chosen Books, 1975), 133-34. Used by permission of Chosen Books LLC, Chappaque, New York. See also Vinson Synan, *Under His Banner: History of Full Gospel Business Men's Fellowship International* (Costa Mesa, Calif.: Gift, 1992), 51-52.

Simpson, A.B.

Charles W. Nienkirchen, *A. B. Simpson and the Pentecostal Movement* (Peabody, Mass.: Hendrickson, 1992), 142-43. Copyright 1992 by Hendrickson Publishers, Inc. Used by permission. All rights reserved.

Stone, Barton

Barton Stone, *The Biography of Elder Barton Warren Stone Written by Himself and Reflections* (Cincinnati: Published by the author by J.A. & U.P. James, 1847). Also see "Piercing Screams and Heavenly Smiles," *Christian History* 45 (XIV:1), 15.

Tomlinson, A. J.

A.J. Tomlinson, "A Journal of Happenings," January 13, 1908. This diary is found in the Church of God archives in Cleveland, Tennessee.

Wesley, John

Vinson Synan, *The Holiness-Pentecostal Tradition* (Grand Rapids, Mich.: Eerdmans, 1997), 4-5.

Wigglesworth, Smith

Stanley Frodsham, *Smith Wigglesworth: Apostle of Faith* (Springfield, Mo.: Gospel, 1948), 44, 104-5. Used by permission of Gospel Publishing House.

Williams, J. Rodman

J. Rodman Williams, preface to "A Theological Pilgrimage." Published online at http://home.regent.edu/rodmwil/. Used by permission of J. Rodman Williams.

Woodworth-Etter, Maria

Maria Woodworth-Etter, *Maria Woodworth-Etter: Her Life and Ministry* (Dallas: Christ for the Nations, 1976), 16, 20, 34-35. Used by permission of Christ for the Nations.